New Testament Handbooks

EDITED BY

SHAILER MATHEWS

THE
HISTORY OF THE HIGHER CRITICISM
OF THE NEW TESTAMENT

NEW TESTAMENT HANDBOOKS

EDITED BY SHAILER MATHEWS

THE UNIVERSITY OF CHICAGO

A series of volumes presenting briefly and intelligibly the results of the scientific study of the New Testament. Each volume covers its own field, and is intended for the general reader as well as the special student.

12mo   Cloth   75 cents each

THE HISTORY OF THE TEXTUAL CRITICISM OF THE NEW TESTAMENT. Professor MARVIN R. VINCENT, Union Theological Seminary.

THE HISTORY OF THE HIGHER CRITICISM OF THE NEW TESTAMENT. Professor HENRY S. NASH, Cambridge Divinity School.

INTRODUCTION TO THE BOOKS OF THE NEW TESTAMENT. Professor B. WISNER BACON, Yale Divinity School.

THE HISTORY OF NEW TESTAMENT TIMES IN PALESTINE. Professor SHAILER MATHEWS, The University of Chicago.

THE TEACHING OF JESUS. Professor GEORGE B. STEVENS, Yale Divinity School.

THE BIBLICAL THEOLOGY OF THE NEW TESTAMENT. Professor E. P. GOULD.

THE HISTORY

OF

THE HIGHER CRITICISM OF THE NEW TESTAMENT

BEING THE HISTORY OF THE PROCESS WHEREBY
THE WORD OF GOD HAS WON THE RIGHT
TO BE UNDERSTOOD

BY

HENRY S. NASH

PROFESSOR OF NEW TESTAMENT INTERPRETATION IN THE
EPISCOPAL THEOLOGICAL SCHOOL AT CAMBRIDGE

NEW EDITION, WITH A NEW PREFACE

New York
THE MACMILLAN COMPANY
LONDON: MACMILLAN & CO., Ltd.
1906

Norwood Press
J. S. Cushing & Co. — Berwick & Smith Co.
Norwood, Mass., U.S.A.

PREFACE

THIS book may seem to be badly planned. Where space is so scanty, to spend four chapters in working up to the critical period that began in the eighteenth century looks out of proportion. Yet the purpose of the book justifies and even compels this procedure. The aim is to make clear to non-professional readers the nature of the Higher Criticism and its divine right within the churches. To do this the history of Bible-study must be followed far into the history of Christianity, even as far as the time when, by the coöperation of the Catholic Church with the moral forces of pagan antiquity, the foundations of modern life and culture were laid, and the Bible was taken to the heart of Europe. Criticism can defend itself before the people only by showing that the history of our religion has made it inevitable. And to do this with any measure of success, the historical causes and conditions of criticism must be treated at greater length than would be seemly if the book were designed for professional readers.

The reader will remember that the aim of the book is not to give a detailed account of the movements of opinion in the field of Introduction. That matter is handled by another book in this series. The aim is rather a philosophy of the history of Criticism.

PREFACE TO NEW EDITION

To borrow a sentence from Hooker, "Dangerous it were for the feeble brain of man to wade far into the doings of the Most High." And it looks like that to venture on an estimate of the fundamental forces of our age, to guess at the direction in which the tides of time are setting, and then to bring one's guess to bear on the nature of the Church's duty in the period that is opening before us. Yet it is possible, by putting together certain main facts and tendencies, to forecast to some extent the drift and movement of history. And if so, it is not presumptuous to draw an inference regarding the task and responsibility of the Church. Our Lord has given her the powers of binding and loosing. Her privilege it is to look into the mind of God and thus to become an interpreter of life for man. She is the Wise Householder in the Master's Parable, bringing forth out of her treasure things old and things new. At every crisis in the history of mankind she is to uncover the foundations of the moral law and to heal the wounded conscience with saving certainty touching the ultimate end and the final issues of our experience. So, to rule the time, she must make herself the servant of the time. And if the logic of history, which for the Church is the will of God, is outlining certain facts with clearness sufficient to enable us to perceive their main lines, then the Church will open her treasure of truth, bringing forth things new as well as things old to gladden and strengthen the heart of man.

One fact, already outlined with a fair degree of clearness, is Nationality. We have barely begun to enter into its deeper meanings. In its final form it becomes a democratic nationality, of the type which America illustrates on so great a scale. What shall Christianity do for the democratic nation ? How keep its fearful force from being brutalized ? How make its unity the servant and not the tyrant of the weak, the critic and not the competitor of imperial ambition ? And how ground its unity ? It is easy for the State's men to be optimistic so long as Democracy has not been searchingly tested. But when the tests become searching, how is the State to be saved from bitter disillusionment ? How is the social will, which is the source of real law, to be made strong and creative ? Only by the self-revelation of the Divine Unity. Here the Nation's unity finds its ground and root. Christianity alone, revealing the unity of the Living God in the depth and passion of human fellowship, can hallow the Nation. And here the Church is to see more and more plainly her work and her duty. It is at this point that Domestic Missions, taken in the largest sense, find their final reason and their decisive test.

And abroad ? The Church is just entering on the greatest debate of her history. She conquered the Mediterranean World by showing herself superior to the other Oriental Religions that were her competitors. But there was one Oriental Religion with which Christianity did not come into close contact, and that was the higher form of the faith that has had its birth and breeding in India. Here the second great fact of contemporary history is disclosing itself. Christianity cannot overcome that Oriental faith by emphasizing the monastic view of life. The sweet and urgent mysticism of India is incomparable of its kind. But the kind is below the level and genius of our faith.

It is through the Christian view of the divine Unity and Personality revealed as the root and ground of the personal and social will making for righteousness, that our religion is to triumph in the great debate. For the ultimate problem of the Race and the Nation is the problem of Law. But in the case of a democratic Nation the problem of law is immensely difficult. It demands the highest and most tenacious form of personal and social purpose. Such a purpose can only be created and maintained by a religion that sets a clear moral end and goal for history and pledges the mind and being of God to its attainment. Foreign Missions, when deeply studied, bring us by another road to the goal of Home Missions. Christianity must manifest its power to build up and support a holy and ministering Nation. This is the final test.

The third fact which is standing out with increasing clearness is the disintegration of the doctrine of infallibility. The infallibility of the Scriptures cannot, in the long run, be separated from the infallibility of the Church. Our Roman Catholic brethren are at this point irrefutable in their logic. If we accept the premiss of Biblical Infallibility, we must eventually have an administrative infallibility to make it something better than a phrase. The doctrine of infallibility is an organism of ideas. It is not possible to permanently detach one part of it from the rest. But concede the Roman Catholic position, and we discover that we have paid an immense price. In order to make administrative infallibility effective, we must have a thoroughly clericalized Church. The Laity may not have any primary part in its government. And then, when the Laity have been driven from the government of the Church, it turns out that the clericalized Church must be a monasticized Church. The picked men and women of our religion, to the end that they may realize the moral ideal, are forbidden to marry. And this means, if we think straight, that Christianity gives up the hope of moralizing the common life. The Family is not holy, in the primary meaning of our terms, and the Nation inseparably joined to the family, is not holy in the highest and deepest sense.

So, if we are to think clearly and to a point, it becomes plain that we purchase our doctrine of infallibility at a very high price. We pay for it with moral scepticism. Can we agree to quiet our understanding at so heavy a cost? Our hearts are set on solving the problem of Democracy. How to make the Nation holy, deserving the utmost sacrifice of her children in times of inevitable war and, — a vastly harder and nobler task, — deserving and receiving their unstinted devotion in times of peace? That is our imperious, our inevitable question. How answer it? Solve the problem we cannot, unless Christianity serve us. But a Christianity that has been monasticized? Will that serve us? Or must we have the Christianity of Christ? What we must have in full measure, if we are to serve the Nation, is a religion that gives us a solid faith, an unswerving and untiring confidence regarding the moral quality and the moral end of history. This the Word of God does. But, to receive the full message of that Word, we must give up our doctrine of infallibility. Then, for the first time, will our Bible have gained its full power of appeal. Its message will become a living word from the living God, winged with power through the life of the Incarnate One, and bringing peace to the hearts of the folk who have dedicated themselves to the wars of God in behalf of a holy Family and a holy Nation.

Therefore the Church of Christ is in honor bound to subject our inherited idea about the Bible to a rever-

ent and unsparing examination. The work, if it be
done grudgingly or of necessity, will not be rightly
done. The Church cannot afford to wait until outsiders force it upon her at the cannon's mouth. She
must herself take the initiative. She alone can do
the work with the patience and the reverent fearless-
ness becoming to a study upon which such incalcu-
lable consequences hang. She must study her Scriptures in the historical spirit. She must discover and
bring to light their human authors. The Old Testament will then unfold itself as a trustworthy book of
witness to the Hope of a Nation chosen to discover
and publish God's deepest method in self-revelation.
The Life of our Lord will be interpreted as the mind
and work of the Head and Leader of the Chosen
Nation who, taking the Nation's Hope for His theme
and His task, purified and perfected it through His
Cross, authenticated and verified it through His resurrection. The Old Testament and the New Testament
together will be studied and read as the book attesting
the holiness of the Nation, and bearing witness to the
Nations that, to preserve themselves, they must become
ministering Nations and, taking the Christ for their
leader and guide, pray and plan for the Kingdom of
God.

When we have gladly given up the idea of infallibility in the interest of the Scriptures themselves,
then we shall expect to find errors and illusions in
the Bible. The mental habits of Antiquity make
errors in matters of science inevitable. The impassioned patriotism of the Prophets makes illusions in
the field of historical perspective equally inevitable.
The conceptions of corporate authorship, widely different from our literary methods, which prevailed
everywhere in Antiquity render certain incoherencies
and contradictions a matter of course. If we judge

the Scriptures in their own light, these things will not surprise or disturb us. On the contrary, we shall joyously accept them as parts of the great plan which has given us our Bible. Without them, the Bible could not have become what it is, the one and sole competent Book of Witness to the quality of God's being and will, the method of His self-revelation and the means whereby earnest people bent upon a sublime task may be saved from sin and melancholy and despair.

St. Ignatius says to Polycarp, " The times call for thee as pilots call for the winds." Is not the Divine Pilot demanding that the Church shall manifest her critical and creative powers? The Nation must be saved from the aristocrat on the one side and from the monk on the other. It is through her ability to guide the Nations toward the Kingdom of God that the Church is to come off triumphant in the debate between the World's religions. Is not free and fearless Bible Study a necessary part of her equipment? Sir Philip Sidney said that the Ballad of Chevy Chase stirred him like a trumpet. When we consider the signs of the times, does not the obligation of reverent criticism become the trumpet of God, stirring our blood?

TABLE OF CONTENTS

CHAPTER I

CHAPTER II

asserts the right of reason to look into divine
truth — The Bible comes into direct contact with
common religious consciousness, and is set up as its
supreme authority — The fundamental idea of Christianity clearly recognised — The Bible shakes off the
bonds put upon it by human opinion — An historical
interpretation of Scripture necessary — Bible-study
ceases to be indirect, through the Fathers and through
Tradition, and becomes a study at first hand.

CHAPTER V

HOW CRITICISM WAS REALISED 77

The eighteenth century — The critical period in the
thought of Europe — Dogma breaks down — Tradition
cashiered — The sacred text set free — By means of
a grammatical and historical method of interpretation
the Bible insures itself against allegorical abuse —
The Bible its own guardian — The human authors of
Holy Scripture come plainly into view — The ideal of
criticism appears — All the records of the past open
themselves to a searching examination.

CHAPTER VI

THE PRELIMINARY WORK OF CRITICISM 100

From Semler to Strauss, 1750–1835 ; — The criticism of the text followed by " Higher " or interior
study — The decay of the ancient conception of inspiration makes a literary study of the New Testament
possible — Problems appear — The relations of New
Testament books to one another are discovered —
The historical movements back of the books are
suggested.

CHAPTER VII

CHAPTER VIII

CHAPTER IX

CHAPTER X

CHAPTER XI

THE HISTORY OF THE HIGHER CRITICISM OF THE NEW TESTAMENT

––––o○⟡○o––––

CHAPTER I

CRITICISM AND INTERPRETATION[1]

LET us fasten our minds on the Bible and take note of the thoughts it gives rise to. We shall find that we are stirred by a deep and lively interest, like that which any great object excites, when it would call us out of ourselves. Our interest runs out toward many things. A mighty and majestic universe has always beset the reason of our race. But it was only a little while ago that we came to know the universe in its true character. Man's discovery of the world he lives in is the commanding feature of the mental life of our time. Nature, having so long and patiently besieged us, has, at last, carried the citadel by storm. The walls are down. Neither indolence nor dogma can longer resist Nature's questions. The results are not all good. Religious folk are sometimes brought into

The first motive of Bible-study.

[1] Literature: The ruling idea of this book being that the Higher Criticism of the N. T. is an integral part of the process whereby the men of the N. T. have come to be interpreted historically, many of the books referred to must necessarily be very general in their character. Farrar, *History of Interpretation*, 1885; Immer, *Hermeneutics of the N. T.*, tr. by Newman, 1890; S. Davidson, *Sacred Hermeneutics*, 1843; Diestel, *Geschichte d. A. T.*, 1869; Hagenbach, *History of Christian Doctrines*, 3 vols. (The Foreign Theological Library); Alfred Cave, *Introduction to Theology and its Literature*, 2d ed., 1896.

deep trouble. Many devout souls, finding the clear
and simple horizons of the old life blurred and
beclouded, are in sore distress. Masses of people
who, in earlier days, would have been under the
influence of Christianity, now wander about as sheep
having no shepherd. These things grieve our hearts.
Still, we cannot turn back the tide of history. The
age we live in, along with its many grievous faults,
has some incomparable virtues. The disinterested
love of truth has never been so strong; nor has there
ever been anything to compare with the wide and eager
study of our time. We have perfected the telescope,
and so broken through the barriers of the skies. We
have developed the microscope until the infinite has
come out of its hiding-place within the familiar.
Above us, around us, beneath our feet, is a world of
objects, all of them interesting, all of them commanding us, with an authority that may not be gainsaid,
to study them and so enlarge our minds.

Bible-study
one of the
mental
interests of
our day.

Dogma, the simple, unhesitating, untiring conviction regarding the things unseen, has greatly weakened. Some day, changed in form, it will regain its
edge and force. For dogma means power and temper
of will, depth and persistence of purpose. And our
age, with the inspiring yet terrible difficulties that
are beginning to confront its choicest ideals, will find,
sooner or later, that it has sore need of dogma. But,
meanwhile, as we wait and pray for a truer and kind-
lier statement of the old faith, we recognise to the full
the intellectual glory and splendour of our epoch. We
are not outsiders to our time. We are within it and
of it. And because we drink deep of its spirit, our
world is full of interesting things, each endowed with
a divine right to be known. The depths of the sea
challenge us to fathom and explore them. The North
Pole does to men what the deed of Miltiades at Mara-

All interest-
ing things
have the
right to be
known.

thon did to Themistocles — it will not let them sleep.
Nature stands before us with a full and eager mind.
To listen to her reverently, to go outside the bounds
of our present knowledge in order to learn new things,
and by learning to enrich and strengthen our race in
its struggle against the conditions that have enslaved
us, this is the ideal of mental life that inspires and
disciplines the highest reason of our time.

To that ideal our minds owe unhesitating loyalty.
Every object that makes a part of our universe calls
to us to come forth from ourselves that we may interpret it.   And we reverently acknowledge the divine
right of the object to challenge us, even though the
time and strength, the faculties and opportunities of
knowledge, be denied us.   Now the Bible is one object
amongst others.   It challenges the reason in us, just
as every great object does.   At the same time, its
challenge has peculiar and compelling power.   For
when reason passes from the high scientific study of
Nature to the scientific study of history; when it sets
out on the search for that self-knowledge which is the
highest form of knowledge; and when, in pursuit of
the deepest self-knowledge, it comes to the history or
autobiography of our race, the Bible comes upon it with
irresistible authority.   In supreme degree it has the
right to be reverently studied.

The Bible has been knit into the experience of the
nations whom God has put in control of the earth.
The story of the way it grew up is at the very heart
of universal history in its ancient period, as that history moved slowly but resistlessly from the earliest
Chaldean Empire to Rome.   The story of its influence
is at the centre of universal history in its modern
period, as that history has marched on from the downfall of Rome to the building of the nations.   It has,
then, a sovereign right to command our attention, a

The Bible
supremely
interesting
because of
the part it
has played

supreme power to tax and control our interest. Think
of it as a book set deep in the best experience of our
race. Then, if we would truly know our responsi-
bilities and our capacities, we must know its story
intimately. Think of it as a literature that has
strongly coloured and shaped the conscience and
imagination of the Occident. As students of literature, we must acquaint ourselves with its intrinsic
qualities and its external fortunes. Think of it as
the book of devotion to high aims and ennobling ends,
from which the choicest spirits of the world have
drawn strength and inspiration. Then, as men of
serious mind, who will not let their science distract
them from their main business — the art of living
nobly — we must study this book thoroughly. That
splendid ideal of knowledge, that impassioned desire
to know, which is the mental glory of our time, lays
upon us the obligation to acquaint ourselves with the
Bible and its history.

The second
motive of
Bible-study.

As we go deeper into our own hearts, we discover
another motive at work. This book, the book of Life
to our fathers, is the selfsame book of Life to us,
their children. As we look at it, warm and joyous
thoughts of the deeds of God visit and cheer us.
Through it the Christ speaks home to us a Word of
God that comes from the depths of the divine Being,
and tells us of a work of God perfectly wrought out in
humanity. We have listened to the Word. The best
that is in us has said "Amen" to Christ's report of
good things. Christ's book has enkindled in us the
sweet and masterful hope that we ourselves may grow
up to the doing of a perfect work. Our reverence for
ourselves, and our trust in our race, bid us reverence
and love the Bible. Our hearts stir us up to study
and know it.

And so, two kinds of piety join their forces to press

upon us the duty of knowing the Bible intimately.[1]
The first is the historical spirit, a true kind of piety,
in that it bids us know the words and deeds of the
men of the past, because of their intrinsic worth and
meaning. The second is the piety of the Christian,
which bids us search the Scriptures because they have
a deeper root in human experience than any other
book, and because they speak home to our hearts as
no other book can. Here are the two great spiritual
desires of our nature working to the same end. There
is, indeed, a vulgar desire to know. Vanity, the
appetite for knowledge that shall have a market value,
the love of fame, the low pleasure of the disillusionment that comes from criticism of the noblest aspects
of the past, these things sometimes stain and soil the
purity of the desire to know. Likewise, there is a
vulgar desire to be saved. The subtle egotism that
pervades many forms of religion, the wish to avoid
complete responsibility for one's own character and
deeds, the base dread of the physical pains of hell, the
low pleasure of feeling one's self spiritually insured,

The desire
to know and
the desire to
be saved.

[1] "Allenthalben widmet man der Erforschung der Alter-
thümer ein Studium das durch eine Art von Pietät belebt wird."
Ranke, *Weltgeschichte*, I, Vorrede. Ranke, after Niebuhr, is
the greatest name in modern historical study. When he calls
the historical spirit a kind of piety, he speaks with authority.
It is indeed a new sort of piety. Its motive is reverence for the
total human past. Its aim is to insure to the men of the past
the right of free speech, so that their words and deeds may retain their individual character, and not be taxed to meet the
needs of feeling or fancy in the present. So the two motives
of modern Bible-study are in unison. The scientific motive demands the original facts and thoughts of Scripture, distinct and
separate from subsequent opinion regarding Scripture. The
religious motive demands the Word of God in its pristine beauty.
The two motives are at one. See also, Keim, *Jesus of Nazara*,
I, p. 4 f.

these things stain and soil the purity of the desire to be saved.

Yet, for all that, these two desires — the desire to know and the desire to be saved — are supreme among the motives that rightfully mould the affections and command the will. The pith of the desire to know is the resolute purpose to see things as they are and to report what one has seen without fear or favour. The pith of the desire to be saved is the holy aim to consecrate one's self as Christ was consecrated, to be perfect as God is perfect, and to work even as He works for the redemption of our race.

The two desires sometimes conflict. Now and then, as we read our Bible, these two desires conflict. Our devotional reading of Scripture is sometimes disturbed by our scientific interest in questions of authorship and history. The scientific endeavour to know the various parts of Scripture in their original meaning and setting is sometimes impeded by our devotional moods. None the less, both desires are at home in our hearts. The Christian in us may not say to the historical student in us, "Thou art of a different spirit; I can have no fellowship with thee!" To say so were to play false to the history of the Occident. Our religion could not have established itself in Europe, unless it had first made its peace with the philosophy of the ancient world. A true victor never wins a victory save through service. The Christianity that conquered the Mediterranean world first served both its mind and its heart. The same law still prevails. By reason of the very frame and constitution of Occidental history, the desire to know is as deep in us as the desire to be saved. The two desires, spite of temporary jars and conflicts, must work side by side in our study of the Scriptures. Otherwise, the Bible will cease to be the Word of Life for men of our kind.

The union of the two motives for Bible-study sug- Union of gests the ruling idea of this book. Holy Scripture the two motives. has the right to be understood. As one great object in a universe of objects, all of them demanding the best effort and the most patient study of the student, it must be known as it is in itself, whether the know-ledge agrees or disagrees with the established opinions of the churches. As the sovereign object of religious study, it asserts the right in supreme degree. Our deep reverence for it forces us to interpret it along the lines of its own meaning and purpose.

It is indeed true that Bible-study, under modern Risks conditions, is attended by risks and sometimes fol- attending modern lowed by losses. A sober-minded scholar cannot Bible-study. think without pain of the many devout souls who cry out, — when criticism shatters some old statement or view, — "They have taken away my Lord, and I know not where they have laid him." No matter how erroneous the statement may have been or imper-fect the view, the pain inflicted by its destruction must needs bring grief to the destroyer. A youthful critic may take pleasure in the use of his apparatus, even as a young surgeon delights to use his instru-ments upon the human body. And sincere Chris-tians, ripe in faith, see things most dear to them, and to many generations of believers before them, handled as intellectual playthings, or at best as a chemist handles elements in his laboratory. The academic thinker is not infrequently far away from the body of the people, and through sheer lack of imagination cannot realise the grief and alarm that criticism is causing. But upon scholars who keep their hearts as well as their heads, these things weigh heavily.

There is something even more distressing. Num-bers of Protestant Christians, although they have neither ability nor equipment for critical study, feel

No sound
conception
of authority.

themselves forced to dip into criticism. They have
no sane conception of authority that can take the
place of the irrational and sacerdotal conception of
the Roman Church. As long as the Bible stood before
their eyes clothed with an infallibility which frowned
down all questions, they lived untroubled. But the
Bible has now come within reach of questions. They
are forced to assume a certain responsibility for the
answers. Lacking the wherewithal of critical study,
yet carried into it by the main forces of the day, they
do not, because they cannot, work at criticism. They
merely worry over it. Criticism enters as a sort of
slow fever into their religion. Their spiritual energies
are grievously wasted.

Certain
losses are
inevitable.

Yet we have read the history of Christianity to little
purpose, if we suppose that the Master of Life will
give us his best things without our paying for them
in grief and trouble. From the beginning, the way
of the cross has been the way of light. We are wit-
nessing, and with or without our will are helping on,
the break-up of that conception of authority and
inspiration which satisfied and controlled the Christian reason for many centuries. Now the undoing of
a great conception, one that has long shaped and
coloured the thoughts of men, is sure to bring some
distressing things in its train. Evil and trouble and
pain have come among us. But we know well that
we are not critics by grace of any human authority.
It is not by our own wish or will that we are what
we are.

The divine
compulsion
in criticism.

The divine will that ever and again drives the
Church out of the old ways and views, to the end that
her eyes may be opened upon new fields of privilege
and duty, is the critic's authority and stay. He
doubts not that a divine compulsion is laid upon him.
And he seeks to persuade the great body of Christian

people that he is ordained of God to defend and make good the rights of God's own Word. If it can be shown that criticism is the inevitable result, the saving necessity of the Church's life, the laity will not be as the children of Ephraim, who, being harnessed and carrying bows, turned themselves back in the day of battle.

It is a commonplace of mental method that we cannot hope to understand the nature of any object, unless we follow it through the stages of its growth. We must know how it became what it is, if we would penetrate its being. This law of method has a force that increases in proportion to the greatness and scope of the object we are studying. The more significant the idea or the ideal that stands before us, the more compelling its claim upon our attention, the less shall we be able to understand its permanent bearings, unless we acquaint ourselves with the story of its growth. Hence, in a matter so significant in itself, and so pregnant with consequences as Biblical criticism, we must follow its history from the beginning.

We must know how a thing grew, in order to understand it.

Since the second century the Christian Scriptures have been deeply and devoutly studied. Why they were studied in one way down to the eighteenth century, and why in our time they are being studied in a different way, constitute a single question. It should be clear that the question can be answered only by a broad appeal to history. And if, through our reading of the history of Bible-study at large, criticism shall be given to us as being both an historical necessity and a divine ideal, we shall all be cleansed of our vanity and fear. The conceit of the critic will disappear when he realises that he is called of God to be a critic. The fears of the layman will vanish when once he is assured that God is holding up before his Church new ideals of life and knowledge. We shall

A broad appeal to history necessary.

be delivered from mental frivolity, — the most hideous of all intellectual faults, — and from that habit of coquetting with criticism upon which Christians of a certain kind congratulate themselves. For criticism will show itself to be the defence of the rights of Holy Scripture, the process through which God is emancipating his Word from servitude to human opinion.

History of Bible-study as a whole.

Nothing short of the history of Bible-study as a whole can achieve this result. If we confine our attention to the years just past — a hundred and fifty, more or less — wherein the "Higher Criticism" has become a distinct discipline, we shall not be able to prove to ourselves that the root of reverent criticism goes as deep as the life of the Church; we shall not wholly allay the suspicion that the Higher Critics are men who, for insufficient reasons, are breaking the peace of the Church. It may be said that, taking the subject so largely, we shall run the risk of losing ourselves. But that is not to the point. Better to be lost than to transgress the law laid down for us by the nature of the subject we propose to take in hand.

The Christian Bible was recognised as Holy Writ during the period that saw the establishment of Christianity as the religion of the Occident.[1]   The

---

[1] Speaking broadly, the building of the Canon is the first chapter in the history of Bible-study. That is clearly the case in the O. T. field. The prophetical literature being the spiritual patrimony of Israel after the Exile, to study and assimilate it, to edit it and to apply it to the needs of the time, became the chief mental and legal training of the Jews. Out of this Bible-study issued the fact and conception of the O. T. Canon. The case is not so clear in the N. T. field. But only because the preëxistence of the O. T. Canon, along with Christianity's speedy detachment from its Jewish base, brought it to pass that the first and decisive steps in the building of the N. T. Canon were quickly taken, when once the need of a N. T. Canon came to be

doctrine of the Canon was built up, not as a thing apart, but as one part of a vast structure of dogma. No one thought of separating the idea of the Bible from the idea of the Church. The two ideas belonged to a single organism of ideas. During the Middle Ages, while the Church's estimate of the Bible's worth kept going higher, still the two ideas clung close to each other. Hence, if we are to take any cognizance of Bible-study before the Reformation, we must read the story in connection with the whole mental life of the Church. Now the part played by the Bible in the Reformation period becomes unintelligible, if we detach it from the history of Bible-study during the mediæval and patristic periods. So, if we take a single step beyond the eighteenth century, we must keep on until we reach the times of the Fathers.

The idea of the Bible and the idea of the Church.

But why should we take that first step? Why not confine our attention to the period of conscious criticism? The specialist in modern Bible-study is tempted to do that. He knows that criticism as an ideal is distinctly a modern thing. It is for the most part in the modern university — and chiefly in the German university — that scientific Bible-study has found both its standing-ground and its apparatus. Why, then, in a book so small as this, attempt to cover so much ground? Why not neglect the comparatively unimportant periods of Bible-study and give all our time to the work of getting clear views concerning the evolution of the critical ideal and methods throughout the professedly critical period?

Specialist's point of view.

There are two sufficient reasons against this procedure. In the first place, we should go wide of our

Reasons against the specialist.

felt. For a brief description of this process, see Muzzey, *The Rise of the New Testament.*

mark. The purpose of the book is to show that criticism is a sacred obligation, a divine calling. We
should have no hope of manifesting this, if we went
no deeper into the history of Bible-study than the
eighteenth century. Criticism must prove that it is
not an alien, not an intruder upon the field of devout
Bible-study; that, on the contrary, it is doing the
same work the Fathers and Scholastics and Reformers
did, and doing it better.

In the second place, we should be disregarding the
nature of our subject, if we took its history so narrowly. Even now, when criticism has fully won the
right of free speech, the Bible is not the critic's book.
It never will be. It is the dearest possession of all
Christians. The critic might as well try to get away
from his own shadow as to get away from the common
Christian feeling about the book to whose interpretation he has given himself. If he does nothing more,
he must at least account for that common feeling, or
else leave himself unexplained. He cannot understand himself without a knowledge of the whole history of Bible-study. There is, then, something better
than a tactical reason for taking our subject very
broadly, although that alone would suffice. There
is a logical reason. The very nature of the subject
forbids our taking its history narrowly.[1]

Accidental
element in
phrase
"Higher
Criticism."

Part of the phrase "Higher Criticism" is a mere
accident. Criticism, in its earliest stage, took the
form of text-criticism. When, at a more advanced

[1] Any view we may take must needs be one-sided. The
critical movement in the life of the churches is one of momentous significance. We ourselves, who attempt to estimate and
assess it, are in the thick of it. If we think ourselves judicial
and "objective," for the most part we deceive ourselves. Our
view cannot but be partial and provisional. We appeal from
ourselves to a later age that shall be better able to judge soundly.

stage, it entered upon the inner study of Scripture, it called itself "higher" in order to distinguish itself from the criticism of the text as a "lower," or preparatory form of study. The adjective is the result of a bare historical incident, having no merit in itself, deserving to be retained — if retained at all — solely on the ground of present convenience.[1]

"Criticism," the other part of the title, is not wholly pleasing. It stirs up needless prejudice, thus partly defeating its own end. A certain kind of mental conceit is often, sometimes not unjustly, associated with the word. On some accounts, "The History of Modern Bible-study" would be a better title than "The History of the Higher Criticism." For "criticism" is one form of Bible-study. The Fathers and the Reformers interpreted the Bible by one method. They were taught of God. We interpret the Bible by another method. We fully believe that God is teaching us. Our study is one with their study in its motive and its reverence. It is superior to theirs, we think, both in its ideal and its apparatus. The term "criticism" is somewhat objectionable. It breaks up the continuity of Bible-study. It sets modern students off by themselves, and repels simple but deep-hearted Bible readers. Yet, for the present, at least, the term is indispensable. It is as significant of our day as the word "evolution." It is not,

Term "criticism" necessary.

---

[1] It might be well to drop the word " Higher " altogether. Devout lay people take offence at it as advertising a superior form of knowledge. If the adjective involved a principle, we should have to retain it, spite of the popular error. But so long as no principle is at stake, it is possibly worth the while of scholars to remind themselves of Rom. 14 : 21. The word " Higher " answers to no present need. It makes neither for clearness nor precision. " Text-criticism " and " Criticism " serve every purpose.

like the adjective "higher," a mere incident of history. On the contrary, it is as necessary to us, just now, as the term "philosophy" was to the Greeks. We must, then, retain it, while taking pains, by our work and behaviour, to commend it.

We shall accomplish our desire, if we can prove that criticism has in view a thoroughly positive end, that back of the critical method which analyses and tests the sources of our information, stands the historical spirit whose aim is to see the past just as it was in itself, to see the course of sacred history — if we may be so bold — as its Author sees it. It will then be plain that criticism is a superior method of interpretation, a better road to the original meanings of Holy Scripture. The exegesis of the Church, from the third century onward, thought of the Bible either as a book of divine law and dogma, or as a book of devotion. Christians went to Scripture to get an answer to the needs of the Church as a thinking, and governing, and praying Church. We have the same needs. But the difference between the old exegesis and the new is this. The old exegesis took the Bible out of its historical setting, and removed it from its relations to definite times and concrete situations, causing the men of the Bible to speak altogether in the language of the men of a far later time. The aim of our exegesis is to find the Bible at home within its history, and, having found it there, to listen patiently and reverently while it tells its story in its own tongue.

Criticism and interpretation.

Definition of criticism.

We define criticism, therefore, as that mental process in modern Christianity whereby the historic character, the true nature, of divine revelation is appreciated and manifested. The historic spirit, the desire to know the whole past even as it was in itself, comes in as a noble servant raised up by God to help the Church to truly know her Bible, and thus pay her debt to the Author of Sacred Scripture. Christianity stands and falls with the Bible. For we believe our Scriptures to be the book of witness to the true quality of ultimate religious experience, and to the character and being of God as revealed through that experience, — the authentic record of the blessed promise and the saving presence of the perfect life on earth. The well-being of the Church depends upon the right interpretation of the Bible. We must seek to know it from within and along the lines of its own meaning and purpose. That is our most sacred obligation.

Well-being of the Church and interpretation.

Criticism is Bible-study, or interpretation, as it must needs be pursued in an historical age. We conceive revelation as a historical process. In order to understand the Bible in its own sense, we seek to find each book of Scripture in its time, and place, and circumstance, and discover the original shape and colour of its author's feeling and thought. The lower, or preparatory criticism aims at the original text, cleared of corruptions and accretions. The Higher Criticism, the original text having been found, aims at the historical interpretation of Scripture. And to study the Bible critically is to assert its right to be understood, to be taken in its own sense.

Criticism true to the Scriptures.

With this definition to guide us, we may venture upon the broad field before us without fear of losing ourselves. Seeing that the old view of the Bible was strongly disposed to take the Bible out of its historical frame, and seeing that the new, or critical, view seeks to put the books of Scripture within that frame, our road is already laid out for us. We are to trace the steps that brought the Church to the point where critical study became an absolute necessity, if the thought and feeling of the Bible were to be rightly apprehended. Then we must consider the conditions

Summary of the history.

that made criticism possible.   And, finally, we shall
try to understand — so far as it is possible for men to
understand a movement whereof their own lives constitute a part — the course taken by the critical study
of the New Testament during the hundred and fifty
years just passed.[1]

[1] While we have no need to remind ourselves of the great
gains of specialism in the N. T. field, it is timely to recall the
dangers.   The old theological "encyclopædia" having fallen
into discredit, the various departments or disciplines of N. T.
study are in some danger of temporarily forgetting their mutual
relations.   Thus Hilgenfeld writes, "Die Isagogik der alten
Kirche war durchaus *hermeneutisch*" (*Einleitung in d. N. T.*,
p. 1).   And Holtzmann to the same intent (*Einleitung*, p. 1).
The terms are not happy.   The fault in the ancient Introductions is not that they are "exegetical" but that the exegesis to
which they contributed was thoroughly unhistorical in its aim
and methods.   If we use our terms carefully, we may say that
Introduction is intrinsically exegetical.   Its purpose is to determine the time, place, author, and relationships of the N. T.
books, to the end that we may enter upon the study of them from
the right or historical point of view.   Nor has a sound Introduction any real surplusage over and above the needs of exegesis.   The appearance of a surplusage is either due to the fact
that a given book is considered too much by itself, apart from
the N. T. as a whole, or else it contains material which might as
well be found in a dozen other places as in a N. T. Introduction.

CHAPTER II

THE BIBLE'S DEFINITION OF REVELATION AND THE
IDEAL OF BIBLE-STUDY THAT GOES WITH IT[1]

WE must not think that the Bible has played a passive part in the history of criticism.   It has been in
large measure its own keeper.   The Old Testament
Scriptures did not lie under the hand of the Jewish
Church, waiting for the opinion of the rabbins to give
them worth.   The New Testament Scriptures did not
lie under the hand of the Catholic Church, until recognition by that Church should insure to them their
standing.

It is, indeed, a common saying that the Church
came before the Bible.[2]   If rightly taken, the saying
contains a helpful truth; wrongly taken, an imposing
fallacy.   The Church did not create the Scriptures.
She appreciated them and recognised their incomparable value.   And her recognition resulted in what
we call the Canon of Holy Scripture.   The destruc-

*The Bible
its own
guardian.*

*"The
Church
before the
Scriptures."*

---

[1] Literature : Sanday, *Inspiration*, 1893, and *The Oracles of
God;* Riehm, *Messianic Prophecy*, 2d ed., tr. 1891 ; Ladd,
What is the Bible ? 4th ed., 1890 ; Maurice, *What is Revela-
tion ?*

[2] This was first said in High Church circles, and was meant
to be an arraignment of Protestantism.   Of late it has been
widely used, in order to lessen the strain of criticism.   If it is
meant to correct the mechanical separation between the idea of
the Church and the idea of the Bible, it is helpful.   But, as
commonly employed, it would be difficult to find a looser statement.

C   17

tion of the Jewish State by the Babylonians, the Exile of the Jews, caused the first step in the building of the Canon to be taken. For centuries the Prophets of Israel criticised and condemned the life of their nation. Their assessments and valuations ran straight against the popular desires and tendencies. The Exile verified their prophecies. Common minds, says Locke, like earthen walls, resist the strongest batteries. The preaching of the Prophets, unaided by external fact, could not have carried conviction with the people. But the Exile brought history over to the side of the Prophets, proving that their words were God's words. Thus the prophetic writings came to be appreciated as their incomparable merit demanded.

The building of the Canon.

So it would be an absurdity to say that, in the pioneer work of building the Canon of Holy Scripture, the Church came before the Bible. The Jewish Church did not create the prophetical books, but admired them, and, by admiration, became capable of appreciating them as they deserved to be appreciated. The Prophets were installed in human opinion as the teachers of humanity. Their word was acknowledged to be God's Word, their criticism of society His criticism, their great hope His personal promise. The Jewish Church was endowed with spiritual perception. And through that perception the prophetical literature canonised itself.

In the building of the New Testament Canon and the formation of the Christian Bible, things took the same course. The Saviour came and fulfilled the prophecies, embodying their words in history and life. His chosen men, filled with his spirit and carried, by his death and resurrection, outside the bounds of Jewish opinion, gave to the world his Gospel, the glad news that God had kept His promise and that the Kingdom of God had been set up amongst men. The

Church of the second, third, and fourth centuries, while, in one sense, identical with the Church of the Apostles, in another sense was distinct. It was one and the self-same Church, just as the Church of our time is one and the self-same Church. If criticism be reverently done, it is a work of exactly the same order as the work done by the Catholic Church when she built the Canon. The Church set the books of Scripture apart from all other books, making them a class by themselves, because she perceived their eternal value as witnesses to the Christ. She appreciated the New Testament Scriptures, and through her appreciation they canonised themselves. And our study, inspired and supported by the desire to see the Oracles of God in their pristine beauty, has the same spiritual quality. We are critics to please the Bible.

Criticism in relation to the Canon.

The saying that the Church came before the Bible, as it is commonly used, can lead only to mental confusion. So far as clear thought is concerned, it either says nothing at all, or it says something that is worse than an out and out error by reason of its specious confusion of error and truth. We cannot affirm that the Church came before the Scripture, if thereby it is meant that the action of the Church gave them their value and authority. Their authority is theirs by divine right, because they are the record of God's self-revelation. Their merit is an intrinsic merit, belonging as truly to them, and to them alone, as the qualities of a triangle belong to the triangle.

The Scriptures do not borrow their authority from the Church.

The Bible has not played a passive part in the history of Bible-study. From the days when the Scriptures canonised themselves down to our own time, they have had a strong hand in the making of their own fortune. As little as the sun is idle before the human eye that gazes upon the beauty of the sunset; as little as the stars are idle when our hearts leap up toward

their splendour, just so little is the Bible inactive
while the Church insures its worth and standing.
The Bible was its own keeper while it was being canonised. It is its own keeper now that it is being
criticised. The "criticising Church" — if we know
and weigh our words — is as noble a title as the "canonising Church." The process of canonising and the
process of criticising the Scriptures have mental and
spiritual qualities in common.[1] Through the former,
God led the world to accept the Christian Bible as
the book wherein we can learn to think about God as
He thinks about Himself. Through the latter God is
teaching men to take the Bible in its own sense.

The Bible criticising itself.

Criticism, then, is not a process thrust upon the
Bible from without. The Bible demands criticism
just as truly to-day as it demanded canonisation in
the third century. For, without modern Bible-study,
the true nature of our Scriptures cannot be fully understood. If it were possible for us to take up the Bible
as we take up the latest book issued from the press,
could we but open it with eyes unvexed by dogmatic
prejudice, we should see at a glance that it is a
thoroughly human book, issuing, as every truly human
document must, from the vital movements of humanity.
So it must be studied as a human book if we would
reach its deepest meanings. In the matter of time it
ranges through fifteen centuries. In the matter of

---

[1] It has already been said that the canonisation of the sacred
books was itself a form of Bible-study. The literature of the
O. T. and N. T. imposed itself upon the religious consciousness
as the standard of religious feeling. The end was accomplished
through study. With this process the critical process has much
in common. For just as the sovereign worth of the Scriptures
forced the world to canonise them, so is the selfsame worth
forcing the Christian reason to know them from within. And
knowledge from within, in contrast with knowledge at second-
hand, is criticism.

feeling it ranges from Samuel, hewing Agag in pieces, to our Lord on the cross, praying for his enemies. But at every point in its range the Bible is deeply human. Samuel is a real man. The Saviour is not less a man, but more. Our Scriptures are not like the Hindoo sacred epics, wherein a great cloudy mist of abstraction settles down upon history, making it look like a mysterious island looming through the fog. The Bible is close to history. The turns of its thought and feeling took place in connection with the great crises of history.[1] It is itself the greatest of histories. It describes a vast mixed movement of human life, through which the creative, redemptive purpose of God shines as the body of heaven for clearness.[2]

Historical study.

Because the Word of God has come to us through the medium of vital history, and not through the broodings and speculations of men who cut themselves off from the common life in order to deepen and clarify their thought, it is rich in colour. The Oriental world stands behind it. The Oriental man lives in it.

For the same reason, it is the book of the common life. The sincerest wisdom of the Hindoos, even the ripest wisdom of the Greeks, is flawed by the distinction between a truth meet for the average man and a truth open only to the religious specialist. The Hindoo and the Greek did not give the world its Bible. That is God's gift and Word to the average man, who does the world's common work and pays the taxes that

Bible not a book for religious specialists.

[1] Riehm, *Messianic Prophecy*, p. 133, 135, 208 ; Baur, *Church History of the First Three Centuries*, I, pp. 1–5 ; Westcott, *The Bible in the Church*, 1893, p. 2.

[2] The O. T. is a better guide than the N. T. into the nature and meaning of revelation. No great idea or conception can be clearly understood, if it is approached only when it is full grown. The O. T. as the book of beginnings, the book mediating between the N. T. and the religions of the world, offers to the student peculiar advantages.

keep its roads in order.   The greatest men of the Old
Testament were citizens and statesmen.   The Master
of men was a carpenter.   His favoured disciples got
no small part of their schooling through the discipline
of a fisherman's life passed upon an exceptionally
stormy and dangerous lake.   The religious specialist
is not found in the ranks of the true men of the Gospel.   The philosopher does not rule in Israel.   God
"hath put down the mighty from their seat and hath
exalted the humble and meek.   The bows of the
mighty are broken and they that stumbled are girded
with strength."   The Bible is the love-story of the
Lord of Life, who meets us in the beaten highway of
history, telling us all that is in His heart.

The Bible not a book of speculation.

Because the Bible is mainly a book of histories, it
is chiefly a book of action.   The men of the Bible are
doers of deeds rather than speculators on thought.
The doubts they meet and wrestle with are practical,
not philosophic doubts.[1]   The dissolving of doubts is
attained not so much through clearer thinking as
through deeper living.   The way of the Scriptures, the
way of light, is not the road of abstract reasoning,
but the road of the cross.[2]   God reveals Himself at
the crises of humanity.   His word and His deed go
together, until His deepest word and His final deed are
brought into unity through Christ.   It is on this
ground that the Bible is called a religion of redemption, — revelation being the story of God's creative
life imparting itself under historical conditions.   The
men of the Bible seek to build up the Kingdom of
God amongst their fellows.   They do not seek to save

[1] Even Job is not a philosophic book in the Greek sense.
The speculative element in the Fourth Gospel has been greatly
overestimated.   The theology of the Bible might fairly be called
Pastoral Theology, in contrast with speculative divinity.
[2] Is. 53 ; 1 Cor. 2 : 2.

their souls by fleeing into the desert. God's life is one of redemptive action. So is theirs.

The men of the Bible are deeply individual, each of them rooted firmly in his time and place. Quite as little as the men of Homer are they personifications of religious abstractions. They are genuine flesh and blood, — the spirit of God shining through their humanity. Their style of speech, their turns of thought are individual. The body of the New Testament, outside the Gospels, is made up of the letters of St. Paul. Now, the law that the style is the man never had a more perfect illustration. His style is himself; it is like no other style in the Bible, as characteristic as the style of Thucydides, or Heraclitus, or Carlyle. The style of the Johannine writings tells the story of an individual life, of an intense nature that has been led through the storms of experience into a childlike simplicity of mind and clearness of intuition. The Bible is a book of individual minds. A single, controlling, divine purpose holds them together. Their books compose into one great book of witness to the reality and the quality of the saving life. Yet each of them is stuck deep in his time and place, as deep as Thucydides, as deep as Shakespeare. Yea, deeper. For each of them took a definite field of human experience for his province, and going to the bottom of the human found the divine.[1]

It follows that the human author plays a very great part in the Bible. If we go to our Bible for our definition of revelation, if we do not first block out and finish our definition in regions of experience more or less remote from the experience of the men of the

Individuality in the Scriptures.

The human authors of Scripture.

[1] The growth of the Scriptures is thus the supreme case under the law governing all catholic or classic literature. Only the books that go to the root of their own time can be a possession for all time.

Bible and then proceed to fasten our definition upon the Scriptures, we shall see that the human author in the process of revelation is indispensable to the Divine Author.   It is not enough to say that the Bible has a human side.   We must say that the Bible is a deeply, an intensely human book.   The little letter to Phile-mon, — from one point of view a mere literary episode, written by the Apostle on the spur of the moment, aimed at a private need, given to the Church from the treasure of a pious family, a fragment out of a life, accidentally picked up and borne along by a great religious movement, — this little letter, rightly taken, becomes one of the most instructive books of Scripture, when once we have made up our minds to take our definition of revelation from no other source than reve-lation itself.   The Bible defines the Bible as a book wherein the Divine Author demands the human author, and bids us see to it that we let not the human author pass out of our sight; lest, perchance, fondly thinking that thus, and thus alone, shall we have a pure Word of God, we deceive ourselves and listen all the while to the echoes of our own words.

The humanness of the Bible, then, is as essential as its divineness.   Herein the book is one with the Christ whose book it is.   And we shall find that the history of Bible-study keeps in step with the history of opinion regarding the person of Christ.   Even as the Church for a long time neglected and sometimes for a while came near forgetting the humanity of our Lord, even so she neglected and almost made light of the human authors in his book.   But if once we clearly understand ourselves as Christians, we shall feel sure that all is over with Christianity, if we per-manently lose or undervalue the humanity of our Lord.[1]   The deepest scepticism of our race lurks

Epistle to Philemon.

The human and the divine.

[1] Dorner's, *Lehre von der Person Christi*, is the best and most thorough treatment of this point.

within the belief that it is impossible for God to come near us, unless we shall first have ceased to be ourselves. Because it is so deep a scepticism, it is wont to palm itself off on less thorough forms of doubt as the deepest truth, persuading men that they must needs abandon the common life in order to find the divine life, that they must go out of humanity if they would take fast hold on deity. But this is not the truth as it is in Jesus. All is lost, if we lose the humanity of our Lord. We slip back from the high and holy ground of revelation into the hopeless morass of speculative heathenism.[1]

Humanity of Christ.

Then the Bible, no longer the book of witness to the simplicity and intelligibleness of God, no longer the book of divine promises touching a Kingdom of God that shall come on earth, no longer the book of that Christ who is humanity's Amen to all the divine promises, — the Bible ceases to be the Bible, the joyous and refreshing study of God's search for us; and adds itself to the number of those great books that tell us the fine yet pathetic story of man's search — the search of the philosopher, and the sage, and the monk, and the mystic — after God.

If, therefore, we would do justice to the humanity of our Saviour, we must do justice to the human and historical character of his book. Criticism, that is to say the kind of Bible-study that seeks an historical

Historical character of Christ's book.

---

[1] One of the most significant debates of our century is that between Mansel and Maurice. (Mansel, *Limits of Religious Thought;* Maurice, *What is Revelation?* *Lives* of Mansel and Maurice.) Heresy makes strange bedfellows. Mansel's idea of God is cognate to Occam's. It requires an imperial, monastical, papalised Church to work it. It practically divorces the ethics of the common life from the idea of God. And it ends by setting up a magnificent clerical establishment which keeps the lay world from throwing the light of reason upon the problems of Biblical study.

interpretation of Scripture, is the Master's personal interest and cause. Without the historical, human book the historical, human Christ ceases to stand out clearly before the eyes of his people. The Bible, therefore, defines revelation as an historical process. With this definition a certain ideal of Bible-study goes along.

Plato, comparing the teaching powers of a book with those of a living teacher, declared that the book is self-helpless, at the mercy of the reader. But this is not true. No great book is at the mercy of its readers. When Plato said so, he was looking at the short run of things. Look to the long run, and his own books prove the contrary. They are his deepest thought eternised, lifted above the changes and chances of the short Athenian day. Students have misread them, carrying into them their own wisdom and ignorance, making Plato speak a language widely different from his own. But only for a while. Sooner or later a great book becomes its own interpreter. Pressing steadily upon the minds of those who love it, it creates at last a true taste for itself. The price the world has to pay for the ownership of a great book is the labour of understanding it. And no matter how long the payment of the debt may be put off, sooner or later it must be paid to the uttermost farthing.

All great books their own interpreters.

So has it been with our Scriptures. Because the Church of an earlier time saw in them a value incomparable, and felt in them a power of God not to be withstood, she canonised them, made of them a Bible. And because the Church of our day, the self-same Church, but living under changed conditions and facing new tasks, has the self-same reverence for them, she is being led into the paths of criticism. In all this mental movement, the Bible does not play a passive part. It is its own keeper.

CHAPTER III

HOW CRITICISM BECAME NECESSARY [1]

IT is the basal idea of Christianity that the Sacred Scriptures, being the book of Witness to the promise and presence of the perfect life amongst men, is the standard whereby the Church must test her doctrine and her life. This does not mean that the Bible alone is our religion, if by "the Bible alone" we mean to take the Scriptures out of relation with the continuous experience of Christians. It does mean, however, that Christian experience, perpetuating and propagating itself through the ages, shall again and again bring itself to book, searching out all possible contradictions between its own ideals and the ideals attested in the Scripture as God's own desire for his people.[2]

The aim of this chapter is to follow the first steps in the history of Higher Criticism by showing how it happened that the Bible, taken away from its history, was interpreted in ways foreign to its own sense.

The basal idea of Christianity.

[1] Literature : Harnack, *Hist. of Dogma* ; Allen, *Christian Institutions*, 1897 ; Moeller, *Church History*, Vol. I ; Westcott, *The Bible in the Church*, 1893 ; *The Canon of the N. T.*, 6th ed., 1889 ; Credner, *Geschichte des neutestamentlichen Kanon*, 1847 ; Loofs, *Leitfaden z. Studium der Dogmengeschichte*, 2. Aufl., 1890.

[2] Briggs, *The Study of Holy Scripture*, 1899, c. 1 ; Macpherson, *Christian Dogmatics*, pp. 24–29 ; Kaftan, *The Truth of the Christian Religion*, tr. 1894, I, pp. 188–202 ; Schaff, *Creeds of Christendom*, III, *s.v.* "Scriptures."

Like inter-
preted by
like.

At the outset we lay it down as a fundamental law of interpretation that like must be interpreted by like. This holds good in the study of single books of the New Testament. There must be a mental and spiritual affinity between the book and the student, if a first-rate piece of exegetical work is to be done.[1] It holds good of the New Testament as a whole. In the long run men think what they are. They will interpret their great text-books along lines parallel with the main motion of their own experience. And if that experience has a different shape and colour from the experience of the men who wrote the books, the books will be misinterpreted accordingly.

Bible not a
sacerdotal
book.

Now the Bible is not a sacerdotal book. It was not written by priests. It is true that the Old Testament contains a large sacerdotal element. But the soul of the Old Testament is that view of the divine and human life which God gave to the world through the Prophets. And as regards the New Testament, along with the other great qualities that distinguish it amongst the " Sacred Books " of the race, this quality is noteworthy, namely, its marvellous freedom from the sacerdotal view of life. Our Master himself was of the tribe of Judah, not the tribe of Levi (Heb. 7. 14). The men through whom he founded the Church and wrote the New Testament were, in almost every case, men of lay birth and breeding.[2] This does not lead

---

[1] This law of spiritual affinity shows itself very plainly when a commentator like Meyer undertakes to cover the entire N. T. While his exegetical methods are the same at every point, the spirit in him answers the mood and purpose of one book better than another. A man who shall write a great commentary on the Fourth Gospel is not likely to do so well with Romans.

[2] The text might have said that this is true without exception. The legend about John's priestly descent is too shadowy to have any value.

us to say that the New Testament forbids the existence of a special priesthood in the Church of Christ. It does, however, justify the assertion that the New Testament, if it would be interpreted in its own sense, cannot permit a body of priests to exercise an exclusive right of interpretation, or anything like it. Through the training and schooling of the Apostles, through the very nature of his book, the Master of Life plainly warned his Church that, if ever she should bring herself to the point where the priesthood should claim such rights, he would put down the usurpation with his own hands, carrying his book into a region of freer life and more generous light.

Criticism, the historical interpretation of the New Testament, became necessary and inevitable when the ecclesiastical doctrine of Tradition carried the Church to a position where her interpretation of Scripture required radical correction. It came to pass that a vast, highly organised and centralised hierarchy claimed to hold in its hands the keys to the meanings of Holy Writ. Their being as a hierarchy was out of keeping with the deepest thoughts of Scripture. Their interpretation, moulded by their being, could not fail to do grievous wrong to the mind of Scripture. Yet they put forward their own interpretation as infallible, — that is, as sufficient, not needing and not open to a searching examination. The ideal of the Church's life demands a true interpretation of the Bible. But the mediæval Church's Tradition was not a true interpretation; it sorely obscured and often destroyed the historical character of the New Testament. The mind of the Church was far away from the original language and the original feelings of the Sacred Books. The human authors of the New Testament passed nearly out of sight.

Hierarchy holding keys of Bible knowledge.

Human authors of Scripture neglected.

The greatest work that men do is often bound up

with great errors.   The Catholic Church could not
have made her wonderful contribution to the history
of Christianity, unless she had developed the dogma
of authority.   It was the growing sense of authority
that gave her strength and coherence, making possible
her victory over the Empire.   It was the same sense
of authority that gave us our Bible.   For without it
we should have had no Canon.   Under the mental
conditions of the time, it was impossible to achieve a
fixed list of Sacred Books by means of historical study.
The spirit of scholarship was too weak, the spirit of
dogma too strong.   Men, as a whole, cared little for
the historic aspect of revelation.   They cared everything for immediate religious certitude and, in case
they had any capacity for speculation, for religious
philosophy.   The Gnostics, against whom the Church
built up the doctrine of the Canon, had no interest in
questions of fact.   Their whole concern was with the
philosophy of religion.[1]   And, beyond question, they
embodied the deepest and freest mental tendency of
the time.   So the Church could not guard herself
against the Gnostics without and the Gnostical tendencies within, by historical investigation.   Nothing
but authority could save the day.   Thus alone could a
fixed or canonic list of Sacred Books be achieved.[2]

Historical
aspect of
revelation
obscured.

[1] A knowledge of Gnosticism is essential to our understanding of the Catholic Church's motives and methods.   For Gnosticism enables us to see what direction the speculative view of
Christianity might have taken, had it not been bridled by Tradition.   Credner, *Canon*, pp. 2–68 ; Harnack, *Hist. of Dogma*, II,
pp. 1–38.
[2] By this it is not meant that there was no historical motive
or element in the process by which the Catholic Church settled
the Canon.   Her traditions regarding the N. T. books were substantially correct (Harnack, *Chronologie der altchrist. Literatur*, 1897, xi).   But the mental bias was dogmatic, rather than
historical.

But with the fixing of the Canon went along the necessity of a fixed and authoritative interpretation of the Sacred Books. The intellectual conditions of the age forbade sound interpretation on any great scale. The allegorical interpretation, in one form or another, was the inevitable tendency of the age.[1] Now, allegory is a system whereby the interpreter can first put any given set of ideas into Scripture, and then, with a grand air of authority, take them out of Scripture. Under the hand of a bold, allegorical method the sacred text lay helpless. To use the blunt speech of a later day, it was no better than a wax nose. The interpreter could shape it and twist it as he pleased.

Philo transformed Plato into an Athenian Moses and Moses into a Sinaitic Plato.[2] The Gnostics found their several systems in our Lord's parables.[3] Even the Catholic interpreters freely allegorised.[4] The

A fixed dogmatic interpretation.

---

[1] The single exception is the "school" of Antioch (Farrar, *Hist. of Interpretation*, pp. 210–218; Kihn, *Theodore von Mopsnestia*, 1880). Strictly speaking, it was not a "school." Theodore was a genius, as far above his time in his scholarship as Aristotle was above his time in his theory of evolution. If Chrysostom and others were exegetically superior to the Alexandrian interpreters, it was not so much because their methods were better as because they had no passion for philosophy. Chrysostom's splendid interest in ethics set him in tune with the N. T.; he had no philosophical system to import into the Scriptures.

[2] Farrar, Lect. 3.

[3] Irenæus (in library of Ante-Nicene Fathers), I, 1, 3. The Gnostics, in dealing with the O. T., were free from allegory and therefore comparatively strong. But they gained their freedom by sacrificing the O. T., and so tearing Christianity from its foundation (Bigg, *The Christian Platonists of Alexandria*, 1886, p. 30).

[4] Justin Martyr did not directly allegorise. But by means of wholesale "typology" he so overrode the historical sense of the O. T. that the difference between him and Philo is hardly

bent and bias of the time was altogether that way. Now, the Catholic Church stood for the common Christian feeling, thought, and law. But if the allegorical method was to be given free play, no widespread community of life and purpose was attainable. Given the allegorical principle, freedom of interpretation meant chaos. Every man would do that which was right in his own eyes. Every school would derive from Scripture a different set of ideas. No broad common ground could be taken and held. Chaos in Bible-study, anarchy in Church government, would have been the upshot.

Prevalence of allegory made this necessary.

If the Catholic Church was to do her great work of subjecting Europe to a common spiritual law, a fixed interpretation was not a whit less necessary than a fixed list of Sacred Books. The grammatical-historical methods of interpretation to which our own period has attained, put the keys to the meanings of Scripture where they rightly belong — in the control of the Bible itself. The well-nigh total lack of such methods in the early centuries forced the Church into her line of action. She insisted upon a fixed and authoritative interpretation.[1]

Historical-grammatical interpretation not possible.

In those days no one dreamed of setting the Bible against the Church or the Church against the Bible. The antithesis would have disabled the Christianity of the period. Even a clear mental distinction, without separation, of Church and Bible would have been untimely. The crying need of the hour was a vast

worth mentioning. If Tertullian and the men of the North African school did not allegorise, it was simply because they had no dogmatic need that drove them into allegory. They had no principles that could have withstood the slightest dogmatic pressure.

[1] Tertullian, *The Prescription against Heretics;* Irenæus, VI, 3, 4 ; Vincent, *Commonitory.*

society held together by common feeling and common purpose. The tactics and discipline of the Roman legion which made the Empire possible, the magnificent capacity of the Latins for law which made the Empire the storehouse of civilisation, was not a bit more essential to the welfare of the world than the splendid coherence, the superb dogmatic drill, of the Catholic Church. The Bible was accepted as the final court of appeal in matters of faith.[1] Upon any other ground the Church would not have been Christian. But there was no thought of pulling Church and Bible apart. The orderly life of the one was assumed to be the indispensable medium of the mind and heart of the other.

Long afterward the clear distinction between the authority of the Church and the authority of the Bible became necessary. At the Reformation the times demanded it. But in the period in which Christianity established itself as the religion of the Mediterranean world, history had no use for the distinction. The

No distinction between authority of Church and authority of Scripture.

---

[1] Irenæus, II, 27 ; 28, 7.

Origen declared that Holy Scripture contained the sum of all the knowledge about God that is attainable in this life. The highest exercise of the sanctified reason is to understand it. (Redepenning, *Origenes*, 1841 ; 1° Abth., pp. 259, 270–272.)

Augustine, *Contra Epist. Man.*, ch. 6 (the famous declaration, "I would not have believed the Scriptures"). But, contending with the Donatists, he insisted on the Scriptures as the supreme authority (II, 3, 4). Theoretically, he leaned toward the ecclesiastical principle (Dorner, A. ; *Augustinus*, 1873, pp. 237–244). But practically, he assumed that the sovereign wisdom of life was embodied in the Scriptures. — Vincent, *Commonitory*, ch. 2, 27, 29. Cassiodorus expressed the estimate of the Bible that passed out of the patristic period into the mediæval period when he described the patristic expositions of Holy Writ as the Jacob's Ladder by means of which men were to ascend to the contemplation of God (*De Inst. Div. Lit., Præf.*).

life of the Church was conceived as a mystical total. It was an organism. Holy Scripture was indeed its heart. But the heart did not say to the hands, "I have no need of thee!" Tradition, the fixed interpretation of an authoritative Church, was thought to be inseparable from a true and saving knowledge of God's Word.

Idea of infallibility.

All the conditions of the period favoured the growth of the ancient idea of inspiration. In like manner they fostered the idea of infallibility. The ideas are inseparable. If the random, destructive work of the sectarian allegorists was to be successfully opposed, if there was to be an absolute, final body of dogma, then the Sacred Books from which the dogmas drew their texts had to be conceived as an infallible body of theological truth. But if it was to be valued as infallible, the human author must go out of it, or, at least, hide in the closet. So the Divine Author of Scripture was left in exclusive possession. When the Biblical student entered the Bible, God alone met him. The doctrine of inspiration tended to remove the Sacred Books from all direct connection with the minds and wills of their authors.

Bible isolated.

The Bible was dogmatically isolated. It could not be treated as a human document. It was held to be inspired. And inspiration, as antiquity conceived it, drew infallibility in its train. So, as an infallible book, the Bible is out of vital touch with reason. For reason exists to ask questions and to insist upon rational answers. But the Scriptures were lifted beyond the reach of searching questions.[1] Reason must kneel, not investigate.

[1] The ancient doctrine of inspiration was shaped in a period when reason was passing into bankruptcy (Windelband, *Hist. of Philosophy*, pp. 210–229).

The inspiration and infallibility of Holy Scripture entailed the infallibility of the Church. Scriptural infallibility without ecclesiastical infallibility is no better than a mighty sword without a mighty hand to wield it. It hangs on a wall as a glorious memory. It cannot do its work. In the long run, the rule-of-thumb infallibility of extreme Protestantism will not serve. The dogma of infallibility, if it is to play an efficient and enduring part in history, must have an infallible Church to translate it into law. Hence, the doctrine of ecclesiastical infallibility developed alongside the doctrine of Scriptural infallibility. It was not, however, systematically elaborated. It lay in the mind of Christendom, awaiting the opportunity for a free career.

Infallibility of Scripture and infallibility of Church.

The opportunity came when the seat of empire was removed from Rome to Constantinople and the emperors lost their hold on the West. Political life, of a high and ennobling order, went off the stage. The State passed into spiritual bankruptcy. The Church of the Occident, thus emancipated from secular control and secured against rival interests, found a field cleared for the development of the sacerdotal principle. And that necessitated the steady exaltation of the Papacy. Mohammed came to the aid of the Popes. His gift was only less helpful than the gift of Constantine. Lopping off from Christendom all the ancient centres of Christianity in Asia and Africa, he insured to the Popes a practical monopoly of spiritual prestige.[1]

The Papacy.

Tradition, as the ancient Church handed the idea over to the mediæval Church, meant a conception of the Bible as infallible, applied to life and carried into practice by a Church believed to be infallible. If, now,

[1] Allen, *Christian Institutions*, ch. 11; also, the standard church histories.

the idea of Tradition was to be logically worked out and carried forward historically into all its consequences of good and evil, a thorough-going centralisation of the Church was necessary.

Centralisation of Tradition.

External history enabled the Papacy to achieve the required centralisation. Down to the eleventh century, all the conditions of the West strongly encouraged the power of Tradition. The success of Tradition depended upon a body of dogmatic interpretations of Scripture pressed steadily upon the mind by a sovereign ecclesiastical authority. Any teacher will tell us that, to have efficient education, we must have concentration of purpose. If a given idea is to take fast hold upon the child's mind, rival interests and pursuits must be kept at a distance. The calamity, the temporary calamity, that sits like a ghost at our modern feast of education, is mental interference. In the primary and grammar schools intellectual persistence is attained. In the high school a crowd of conflicting attractions rush upon the mind, and the capacity of attention is dissipated. The multiplication of interests makes steady pressure of any sort a thing very hard to get.

The classic period of Tradition.

But mental concentration was the natural tendency in the early Middle Ages. The poverty of interests gave the principle of Tradition full sway. The cities of the West had fallen into ruins. Now, we know that throughout antiquity the city, in opposition to the country, was the place where mind rubbed against mind, where impressions jostled each other, where ideas moved and changed. The country was the place where the mind handed on, without alteration, the views it had obtained from the past. In the modern world, the antithesis does not hold good; because the marvellous mechanical inventions of our age have largely conquered space. But in the ancient and the mediæval world, it held true, without exception, that the city was the place where, by reason of the conflict of impressions and the collision of ideas, a single idea found the most difficulties in the way of its making a permanent fortune. The countryman's life and conditions fostered conservative views and gave an easy monopoly to any strong and persistent conception.[1]

The cities were in ruins, commerce at a standstill. The great public and private libraries of the Roman world had perished. It was not possible that there should be any large and free mental life. It is true that the monasteries earned the undying gratitude of scholars by giving a safe asylum to literature. Against the attacks of barbarous men, and the pressure of barbarous times, they maintained the continuity of mental life. None the less, mental life was at a low ebb. The scope of the mind was narrow. The quantity of knowledge was small.[2] The desire to know filled a comparatively small space in the field of attention. The pressure of facts on the mind was slight. The times were free from mental interference. Tradition throve.

External conditions.

Everybody knows that the mental conditions of our own period are fundamentally different. The uni-

Contrast with our time.

[1] Sparta and Athens are the contrasted types in Greek life; Palestinian and Alexandrian Judaism in Jewish life. Droysen brings out the function of the city in the economy of the ancient world, in his masterly *Gesch. d. Hellenismus.* It was not an accident that made Alexandria the centre of the religious speculation of the Empire (Windelband, *Hist. of Philosophy,* p. 213).

[2] The history of the map of the world is a good index to the shrinking or enlarging body of earth-knowledge. Beazeley, *The Dawn of Modern Geography,* 1897; Fiske, *Discovery of America,* I, ch. 3.

A trustworthy witness to the state of mental productivity down to the year 1000 is found in the statistics of exegetical work (Schaff, *Hist. of the Christian Church,* IV, p. 602).

verse, whose infinitude and majesty we have just begun
to discover, presses resistlessly upon our minds. The
whole world, for the first time made one, sends a vast
body of conflicting ideas and conceptions against all
established ideas. Many sore evils follow. Faith
lacks stability. The spirit loses its simplicity. Clear
vision is often obscured. Creeds are as wax in the
hands of circumstance. Believers drift without sail
and anchor, or lie on the flats. But the gain far out-
weighs the loss. The infinitude of truth becomes a
passion. On all sides we hear the wind of God blow-
ing. And we know that we do not know whence it
comes and whither it goes. Humility becomes, in
the realm of the mind, the same cardinal virtue it has
always been in the sphere of Christian ethics. Our
minds are kept open to the new things that God has in
store.

Ideas fixed.

How unlike the early Middle Ages! The men of
that time had no appetite for the learning that lies
remote from narrow, practical ends. They altogether
lacked our lively feeling for a world of things standing close to knowledge, although not yet come into
knowledge. They had no eager sense of the truths
that stand at the door and knock.[1] Free from severe
mental pressure, the ruling ideas became stiff and
unelastic. In the absence of an expanding knowledge, there was no need to reconstruct interpretations.
The principle of a fixed, authoritative interpretation
of Scripture found everything to its liking.

Bible iso-
lated in
a double
sense.

The Bible was now isolated in a double sense. It
had been dogmatically isolated by the ancient Church,
through the doctrines of inspiration and infallibility.

---

[1] The text does no injustice to scholars like Bede and Eri-
gena. They had a profound sense of the majesty of divine truth.
But their knowledge came to them along the line of Tradition.
There was no mental competition.

Jerome's dream illustrates this. "How can Horace go with the Psalter?" he writes, "Virgil with the Gospels, Cicero with the Apostle? . . . Many years ago, when for the kingdom of heaven's sake I had cut myself off from home, parents, sister, relations, and, harder still, from the dainty food to which I had been accustomed; and when I was on my way to Jerusalem to wage my warfare, I still could not bring myself to forego the library which I had formed for myself at Rome with great care and toil. And so, miserable man that I was, I would fast only that I might afterward read Cicero. After many nights spent in vigil, after floods of tears from my inmost heart, after the recollection of my past sins, I would once more take up Plautus. And when at times I returned to my right mind, and began to read the Prophets, their style seemed rude and repellent. I failed to see the light with my blinded eyes; but I attributed the fault not to them, but to the sun. While the old serpent was thus making me his plaything, about the middle of Lent a deep-seated fever fell upon my weakened body, and while it destroyed my rest completely, — the story seems hardly credible, — it so wasted my unhappy frame that scarcely anything was left of me but skin and bone. Meantime, preparations for my funeral went on; my body grew gradually colder, and the warmth of life lingered only in my throbbing breast. Suddenly I was caught up in the spirit and dragged before the judgment seat of the Judge; and here the light was so bright, and those who stood around were so radiant, that I cast myself upon the ground and did not dare to look up. Asked who and what I was, I replied, ' I am a Christian.' But he who presided said: ' Thou liest; thou art a follower of Cicero, and not of Christ. For "where thy treasure is, there will thy heart be also."' Instantly I became dumb, and

Jerome's dream.

amid the strokes of the lash — for he had ordered me to be scourged — I was tortured more severely still by the fire of conscience, considering with myself that verse, 'In the grave who will give thee thanks?' Yet for all that I began to cry and bewail myself, saying, 'Have mercy upon me, O Lord; have mercy upon me.' Amid the sound of scourges this cry still made itself heard.   At last the bystanders, falling down before the knees of him who presided, prayed that he would have pity upon my youth, and that he would give me space to repent of my error.   He might still, they urged, inflict torture on me, should I ever again read the works of the Gentiles.   Under the stress of that awful moment I should have been ready to make still larger promises than these.   Accordingly, I made oath and called upon his name, saying, 'Lord, if ever again I possess worldly books, or if ever again I read such, I have denied thee.'   Dismissed, then, on taking this oath, I returned to the upper world, and, to the surprise of all, I opened upon them eyes so drenched with tears that my distress served to convince even the incredulous.   And that this was no sleep nor idle dream, such as those by which we are often mocked, I call to witness the tribunal before which I lay, and the terrible judgment which I feared.   May it never hereafter be my lot to fall under such an inquisition! I profess that my shoulders were black and blue, that I felt the bruises long after I awoke from my sleep, and thenceforth I read the books of God with a zeal greater than I had previously given to the books of men." [1]

[1] It would not be safe to take Jerome literally.   By nature he was a religious impressionist, a lover of the luxury of feeling. And he associated with devout women more than was good for him.   Yet, after the necessary discount is made, his "dream" is typical of the tendency in the Western Church.   No scholar of

Jerome's dream shows how the Scriptures were dogmatically isolated. Between the fifth and the twelfth centuries circumstances operated powerfully in favour of practical isolation. The desire to know, scientific curiosity, existed, but that was all. The motive of knowledge was weak, the materials scanty. Even the knowledge about the authors and circumstances of the New Testament books had shrivelled to a bare handful of facts.[1] This small body of information was considered sufficient. It had the prestige of a sacred antiquity and the authority of an infallible Church to guarantee it. Men felt no desire to go beyond it. They lacked the motives that should lead them to study the New Testament as a history. They lacked the knowledge that holds our idea of the Bible close to the ground of a human and historical process. So the isolation of circumstances came to the help of the dogmatic isolation of Scriptures. The Bible was separated from human literature by forces external as well as by forces internal. It was cut off from the possibility of historical investigation.

Owing to this twofold isolation of Scripture, it

Little scientific curiosity.

the Greek Church could have had such a dream. The suspicion of pagan learning became deep-seated. "It was the custom among some monks, when they were under the discipline of silence and desired to ask for Virgil, Horace, or any other Gentile work, to indicate their wish by scratching their ears like a dog, to which animal, it was thought, the pagans might be reasonably compared" (Lecky, *Hist. of European Morals*, Appleton, 1877, 2, p. 203). Boccaccio was badly frightened (about 1360) by a monk who foretold his speedy death and bade him give up his classical studies (Raumer, *Gesch. d. Pädagogik*, I, p. 16).

[1] The student should read Cassiodorus in order to get an idea of the narrow range of the information regarding the N. T. books in the Western Church after the sixth century. Yet, such as it was, it gave entire satisfaction. The mind rested on it.

Immuta-
bility.

came to pass that the idea of change or process in connection with the New Testament lay outside the range of ecclesiastical opinion. The scholars of the ancient Church were well aware that there had been differences of opinion concerning the canonical standing of various New Testament books. The familiar words of Eusebius will bring this clearly to mind. He distinguished between the books of an unquestionable standing and those whose standing was in doubt.[1] He knew, as Jerome and other scholars knew, that the Latin and Syrian and Alexandrian churches were not of one mind upon some important points.[2] And the most elementary study nowadays brings to us the knowledge that the Christian Bible was not made at a stroke, that the New Testament literature did not come fully level with the Old until the end of the second century, and that the process of canonisation lasted for two centuries.

Ancient dif-
ferences of
opinion for-
gotten.

But all this knowledge lay outside the ken of the Middle Ages. The Canon was thought of as a deed of God, done at a stroke. The human authors of the New Testament books were out of sight and mind, and, with them, all sense of the special occasions or the particular aims of individual books. The thought of change or process either within the New Testament or in connection with it was wholly foreign to the student of the Bible. The Canon of the Scripture stood before the mind's eye as a divine immutable total.

The mediæval Church had also lost the scientific

[1] Eusebius, *Church History*, III, 3, 25 (McGiffert's *Translation and Notes in the Nicene and Post-Nicene Fathers*, 1890). Until the sixteenth century these facts were practically sunk in oblivion.

[2] Bleek, *Introd. to N. T.*, II, pp. 263, 269, 272 *sq.* ; Hilgenfeld, *Einleitung in d. N. T.*, p. 123.

apparatus for Bible-study. The ancient Church could show a noble band of scholars, some of them great both in spirit and in method. The text-criticism of Origen and Lucian, the Commentaries of Theodore and Chrysostom, the historical studies of Julius Africanus, the labours of Jerome, deserve high praise. These men had direct access to Scripture. All of them knew the Greek. The Syrian scholars, and Jerome as well, knew the Old Testament in the original. The Bible-study of the ancient Church was, in large measure, direct study. It used the original languages of Scripture. It stood close to the original sources of information.

Lack of scientific apparatus.

But in the Middle Ages the scientific apparatus for the direct study of Scripture was very largely lost. The knowledge of the Greek kept up a meagre and precarious existence.[1] Hebrew, so far as practical use went, was lost altogether.[2] The Latin text, called the Vulgate, was supreme. What with ignorance, and piety, and habit, — a mighty triumvirate, — men did not feel called to go behind it.[3]

Direct knowledge of Scripture not possible.

There is a well-known kind of sloth that gladly finds an asylum in religion. So subtly do the noble and base elements in humanity intermingle, that the

[1] " *Græcum est, non legitur,*" nearly covered the ground. The greatest thinker of the Middle Ages, Thomas Aquinas, knew Greek, but his knowledge was neither full nor sure.

[2] Bede knew a little Hebrew (Giles, *Bede's Works*, 1843, I, p. li). But like Philo's knowledge of the meanings of Hebrew names, it was just enough to be a snare. The Council of Vienna (1312) urged the establishment of chairs of Hebrew at Paris, Oxford, Salamanca, and Bologna (Geiger, *Joh. Reuchlin*, p. 103). But nothing of account came of it.

[3] There were good reasons for the supremacy of the Vulgate. The devotions, the Canon Law, the liturgical usages of a thousand years, the universal value of Latin as the language of educated men, worked toward this end.

holiest things are sometimes made the cloak and cover
for the meanest.   Piety often stands hard by mental
laziness.   So the ignorance and inertia of the period,
using the noble name of religion, accumulated upon
the sacred text a great mass of traditions, coming
indeed from various sources, yet all claiming the
highest authority, even the authority of Holy Writ.
Inertia and religion. The monks of Sinai, in course of time, placed within
easy walking distance of their monastery all the sacred
sites associated with the giving of the Law.[1]   When
scientific curiosity and mental stimulus were absent,
it was inevitable that they should introduce men to
sacred things along the line of least resistance.   This
illustrates the way in which mediæval piety frequently
went to work in order to acquire its knowledge of the
Sacred Books.

Even when Biblical students were like Bede, strenuous and eager, the lack of data was a fatal handicap.
A first-hand knowledge of Scripture was impossible.
This condition of knowledge concerning the Holy
Land is a good example of the prevailing ignorance
regarding Biblical realities.   Palestine was covered
deep with a thick stratum of Western traditions
which, in a majority of cases, had lost all connection
with the traditions of the country as well as with the
text of Scripture.   The land where the Sacred Books
grew up, although under the feet of pilgrims and
monks, ceased to be a witness to the meanings of the
Bible.   Foreign opinion and foreign ignorance had a

[1] Palmer, *The Desert of the Exodus*, I, p. 8: "All the most
interesting sites" were grouped "within an hour's walk of the
Convent of St. Katherine."   Adam Smith, discussing the low
state of learning at the English universities in his time, observes,
"It is the interest of every man to live as much at his ease as
he can" (*Wealth of Nations*, bk. 5, ch. 1).   The remark has a
wide bearing.

free hand.   The established ecclesiastical interpreta- Ecclesiasti-
tion of Scripture had the same free hand.   Antiquity cal interpretation has
was indeed reverenced as the seat and source of its own way.
authority.   But antiquity, so far as clear knowledge
went, was largely an empty field open to preëmption
by pious fancy or dogmatic interest.[1]

Furthermore, the ecclesiastical Tradition of the
West had a peculiar power.   Compared with it, the
Tradition of the Eastern Church was a body without
a head, deficient in clear self-consciousness and in
capacity for self-direction.   The idea of ecclesiastical
infallibility — that idea without which Scriptural
infallibility could not be successfully applied — could
not attain in the East a logical evolution.   In the
West this was possible.   The Papacy provided the
organ that was needed.   Now, the doctrine of Tradition presupposes the belief that the Church is infallible.   Just in proportion as this belief takes itself
seriously, does Tradition become masterful.   So,
through the triumph of Rome, Tradition came under
the control of a hand capable of directing it to definite
ends.   The papal authority became the centre of the
entire body of traditional interpretations of Scripture.
The Popes held the power of the keys.   They could
bind and loose.   It was for them to determine how the
Bible should be understood.[2]

What was the mental quality of the Tradition or Mental
interpretation that laid its hands on the sacred text quality of
ecclesiasti-
with an authority so self-possessed and so command- cal interpretation.

[1] Reverence for antiquity, if not chastened by the scientific
desire for knowledge and checked by a large and lively body of
facts, always acts in this way.   For an illustration close at hand
see Lodge's discussion of the stories about Washington's boy-
hood.   Yet America is the least likely place in the world for
legendary growths.

[2] Luther's address to the German nobility.

ing?   We have seen that, in early centuries, Tradition was the sole means of bridling the allegorical
exegesis; that, without it, the New Testament would
have been helpless in the grasp of any philosophical
system or theosophic view that happened along.   For,
since the grammatical and historical method of interpretation had not been reached, the Bible was not
permitted to tell its story in its own tongue.   Therefore, just as the Church gave us our Bible by insisting on a fixed list or canon of Sacred Books, so she
preserved for us our spiritual heritage by dogmatically ruling out the multitudinous Gnostical interpretations which would have shattered her unity and
unfitted her to train and tutor the strong but barbarous nations of the West.

The Church was true to the Bible.   Under the
conditions of the time, there was no other way to
appropriate and hand down God's saving Word —
the revelation of the human unity that is to be built
up on the divine.   But in the course of a thousand
years it came to pass that the dogmatic tradition of
the Western Church, thanks to deep ignorance on the
one side and to an imperious confidence in its own
finality on the other, imprisoned the sacred text which
in the old days it had guarded.[1]

Little
knowledge
of Greek
and Hebrew.
Knowledge of the original languages of Scripture
being at a minimum, the main body of information
concerning the books of the Scripture — their authors,
their times, and places — having sunk into forgetful-

---

[1] One of our needs is a thorough study of the Bullarium as a
contribution to the history of interpretation.   Nowhere else is
it made so plain that the interpretation of the Middle Ages was
based, not on the nature and qualities of Holy Writ, but upon
the will of a vast institution.   Rashdall well says that the
mediæval mind had a peculiar genius for embodying its ideals
in institutions (*Universities of Europe in the Middle Ages*, 1895,
I, p. 5).

ness, it was easy for a dogmatic or mystical exegesis to run a free course.[1] And this was the universal exegesis of the Middle Ages.[2] Philology had not yet come to create in Christian scholars a sense for the solidity of the laws that govern language. History had not yet brought in a commanding body of facts to check and restrain the will of an imperial Church. In one way or another, under one form or another, allegory was the established, the authoritative method of interpretation. The dogmas of the Church, received upon authority, kept chaos from breaking forth upon Bible-study. But in the course of a thousand years, dogma itself travelled far from the original feeling and thought of Scripture. The historical meaning of God's Word was grievously obscured.

The Church that now imposed her interpretation upon God's Word headed up in the Papacy. The dogma of infallibility was already entering the last stage of its history. Looking forward from the towering claims of the great mediæval Popes, the Vatican Council of 1870 is in plain view.[3] The belief in the

Dogma of infallibility centralised.

[1] Upon the relation of the mystical interpretation to the dogmatic interpretation and the relation of both to the historical nature of Christianity, see Dorner, *Protestant Theology*, 1867, pp. 1–59.

[2] The mediæval interpretation of the N. T. was superior to the interpretation of the Old (Rosenmüller says this of Bede, *Hist. Interp. Lib. Sac.*, 1795–1814, vol. 5, p. 92 *sq.* It might be said at large). This was a happy accident. In an age that lacked the idea of evolution, the O. T. had a far stronger need of the allegorical interpretation.

[3] The fourteenth and fifteenth centuries were times of dogmatic relaxation. The rally and revival of mediævalism in the sixteenth century sketched the modern conception of the Papacy at the Council of Trent. In the eighteenth century came another period of relaxation. But the religious revival of the nineteenth century carried the Papacy straight on to the Vatican Council of 1870.

papal supremacy and the papal infallibility were on the verge of being regarded as essential to salvation. And the Church taught that all this could be found more or less clearly in God's Word.

The temporal power of Papacy.

The Church that read her own mind into Scripture had become a vast political establishment claiming dominion over kings and peoples. The Pope took it upon himself to crown and to discrown monarchs. He laid his hands on Magna Charta. And all this under the guise of an infallible and final interpretation of texts like "Thou art Peter" and "Here are two swords."

The Church that claimed the power of the keys, the sole and exclusive right to interpret Holy Scripture, had become an out and out monastic Church. And if ecclesiastical infallibility is to be effectively used; if it is to be anything better than a cloudy abstraction wherein the mind, pursued by difficulties, hides itself from its pursuers; if it is to be a working institution, this must always be the course of things. There must be a body of men who shall be as unlike common human society as it is possible for men to become while remaining upon the earth and existing as a society. They must have a constitution fundamentally unlike the constitution of laymen. In lay society men and women marry, calling upon God to help them cleanse their love from lust that they may build up holy families. But the men and women who constitute the inner circles of the infallible Church cannot marry. In lay society the individual holds property, calling on God to help him use his money for the good of others. But the men who constitute the governing body within the infallible Church cannot have any property of their own. In the lay world men insist upon their right to know and govern themselves, to think freely, and to speak freely. Only in

The Church monasticised.

time of war do they subject themselves to martial law.
But at the heart of the infallible Church a different
ideal holds sway. The control of the Church is in the
hands of a society, like the Jesuits, which sets up the
martial law of absolute obedience as the type of law,
and in which the individual must put his will at the
feet of the institution, making himself will-less like
a corpse. And all this had to be, if ecclesiastical
infallibility was to really work. The right to govern
and to think in the Church, the right to claim, in the
full sense, the ideal of holiness, must be vested in a
vast, undying corporation, in a close-knit body of
priests, whose members are detached from the lay
world by the vows of poverty, and chastity, and obedience. Moreover, the confirmation of all this, if not
the authority for it, must be found in Scripture. For
the Church all along was loyal, in purpose and
motive, to God's Word. The sovereignty of the
Scriptures was practically, if not theoretically, taken
for granted. Tradition was indeed sacred, and the
Bible could not be understood apart from Tradition.
But the sincere and devout assumption was that it
interpreted the Bible aright.[1] So it was necessary to
find in the sacred text the entire conception and
scheme of the monastic and infallible Church. A
non-grammatical, unhistorical exegesis carried the
Pope and monastic establishment into the Scriptures,
— into that Old Testament which is the book of Witness to the inspired thoughts of men who lived out
their lives within the bounds of a nation's experience,
and into that New Testament which is the book of

*A large body
of foreign
opinion
imposed on
Scripture.*

---

[1] The history of the doctrine of Tradition in its relation to
Scripture still remains to be written. H. J. Holtzmann's *Kanon
u. Tradition*, 1859, is a strong book, but almost wholly on dogmatic lines.

E

a Son of God who made himself like unto us in all things, sin only except.

Thus the mediæval Church fell into deep self-contradiction. Her main desire was to know God's Word truly. Erigena prayed thus with himself, "O Lord Jesus, no other reward, no other blessedness, no other joy ask I of thee than this — that I may be freed from the error of my own speculation and know thy words in their purity." [1] All the saints and leaders of the mediæval Church prayed so. By their study and thought they exalted Holy Scripture. The great Popes stopped the mouths of their adversaries with a text. The Canon Law rested upon the Bible as an ultimate authority. Everything of high degree in the Middle Ages joyously paid tribute to the majesty of the Scriptures.

Indeed, as one century followed another, the spiritual prestige of the Bible rose higher and higher. The longer the reign of Tradition lasted, the more precious, in the eyes of the Church, did the Scriptures become.

Church contradicts her own idea.

But the doctrine of ecclesiastical infallibility shut the Church up within a circle from which she could not break forth. An infallible interpretation, if it means anything worth speaking of, means a sufficient interpretation, not only sufficient for the needs of the contemporary Church, but also satisfactory to the sacred text itself. Now the doctrine of infallibility — no longer loose-jointed as in earlier days, but, thanks to the Papacy, compact and masterful — gave large satisfaction to certain governmental and devotional needs of the Church. It did not, however, and it

[1] Hagenbach, *Dogmengeschichte*, 5ᵉ Aufl., p. 354. The letters of the great Popes, Hildebrand and Innocent, and of saints like Bernard, show how truly this noble prayer expressed the deepest desire of the Middle Ages.

could not meet the demands of the Bible for an interpretation along its own interior lines. On the one
side, a human interpretation of the Word was installed
as its keeper. And so the fortunes of the Bible were
bound up with the fortunes of Tradition. An attack
upon Tradition turned into an attack upon God's
Word. On the other side, the authoritative interpretation was not open to searching criticism.

The established interpretation of Scripture could,
of course, be changed. Necessarily, an institution so
vast as the mediæval Church, including and satisfy-
ing so many interests, has its laws of development.
But the changes were indirect and roundabout, made
under cover of legal fictions.[1] The very changes, so
long as they were covered by the fiction, not frankly
recognised as the correction of errors, gave a longer
lease of life to the original error, the doctrine of ecclesiastical infallibility. As a result, these indirect cor-
rections of false interpretation could not lead the
Church toward the true goal of Bible-study, namely,
the insurance of the right of Holy Scripture to be
interpreted in its own language and in its own sense.

Here, then, the Church fell into a grievous internal conflict. The Bible was the centre and heart of
the Church's collective testimony to God's view of
man's life and His own. It was a supreme, if not the
supreme, object of faith. As such, it possessed, in
the highest degree, the right of all great objects —
the right to be understood. And the Church loyally
conceded the right. But at the same time, by her

*The Scrip-
tures not
allowed to
interpret
themselves.*

---

[1] Upon the vast part played by legal fiction in the building
and maintenance of institutions, see Maine, *Ancient Law*, ch. 2.
There is a large element of legal fiction in the conception of
papal infallibility. The discussions concerning the notes that
distinguish the Pope speaking *ex cathedra*, from the same Pope
speaking on a lower level, prove it.

The supreme question postponed.

efficient governmental application of infallibility, she made it impossible to put the ultimate question of Christianity fairly and to force it home. What is Revelation? what its nature and method? is our ultimate question. The appeal to the Church's infallibility merely puts the question off.

No great question can be settled by being put off. With every postponement the debt to reason and conscience grows heavier. Sooner or later, the debt must be paid, and paid in full. The Bible could not be permanently pent up within Tradition. Its breaking forth was only a question of time. To be true to itself, it must come within reach of the lay reason, and into direct touch with the conscience of the lay world. The choice before the Bible lay between a splendid isolation and imprisonment within Tradition, on the one side, and, on the other, criticism with

Criticism essential to the Scriptures.

all its risks and dangers. In the light of the Bible's own nature and history, but one choice was possible. The Scriptures must choose the path of free criticism, under pain of not being known as they are.[1]

---

[1] The grip of this dilemma cannot be loosened. Were the entire Protestant world to enter the Roman communion to-morrow, the "Reformers before the Reformation" would straightway begin their work again, and Holy Scripture would insist upon bringing Tradition to book.

CHAPTER IV

HOW THE POSSIBILITY OF CRITICISM WAS GIVEN [1]

So far, the history of criticism runs as follows: The Scriptures of Israel and of Apostolic Christianity, by their own intrinsic merit, were able, in the course of the second, third, and fourth centuries, to canonise themselves in the mind of the Catholic Church, thus becoming the Sacred Books of Christendom. While this was happening, they were being tied up with traditions and doctrines not altogether to their liking. In the following centuries, by reason of the hard times, the decay of lay learning, and the weakness of the State, the Church was led to take her own infallibility with deepening seriousness and to apply it with increasing efficiency. Tradition set itself up as a sufficient interpretation of the Scriptures, while assuming a grand air of finality. Through the development of the Papacy and the resulting centralisation of Church institutions, Tradition tightened its hold on the sacred text. Yet, all the while, by isolating the Scriptures, by keeping them remote from reason, and treating them as if they were altogether above reason, the Church exalted their value in the eyes of the self-same laity who were denied the right to interpret

[1] Literature: Ranke, *Hist. of Germany in the Period of the Reformation*, I; Luther, *Primary Works* (tr. by Wace and Buchheim); Moulton, *Hist. of the English Bible*, 1878; Schaff, *Creeds of Christendom*, III; Dorner, *Hist. of Protestant Theology*.

them. The longer the isolation and prohibition lasted, the more powerfully did the Scriptures strain at the cords of Tradition. It was inevitable that, sooner or later, the Bible should break away from its keeper.[1]

And now we are to see how, from the one side, the laity pressed in to touch the most sacred things with their own hands, while from the other the Bible went forth to meet them. Hereby the death knell of the allegorical exegesis was rung. That the Bible should be interpreted as a human book became only a question of time. For, taken to the heart of the laity and lying open in their hands, it must needs be studied as the lay reason studies other things — through free questioning and through scientific investigation.

The Bible must be treated as a human book.

So long as the interpretation of Holy Scripture remained in the hands of ecclesiastical infallibility, Bible-study could not be thorough. The appeal to the authority of the general councils, the appeal to the Fathers, the appeal to the Popes, all had their value.

[1] Marsilius of Padua put forth (about 1324) the *Defensor Pacis*, as a plea for the Emperor against the Pope. With great clearness he affirms the sovereignty of Scripture (III, 2, 1). Christ is the sole judge in things divine (*Christus . . . nullus alius*, II, 9). Nothing deserves unconditional belief save Holy Scripture, and the interpretation is to be *communi concilio fidelium*. (In Melchior Goldasti, *Monarchiæ S. Romani Imperii*, 1668, II.) A study of the other political treatises contained in the three volumes demonstrates that the theoretical emphasis upon the rights of the State, growing steadily from the thirteenth century on, worked for the depreciation of Tradition as a clerical monopoly, and for the exaltation of the Scriptures. See, also, Wiclif, Preface to *De Dom. Div.*, and Lechler, *Wiclif*, I, pp. 467–489. While the political life of the Occident was thus loosening the connection between Scripture and Tradition in one way, the devotional needs of Christendom were loosening it in another (Ullmann, *Reformers before the Reformation*, I, pp. 8, 54 ; II, pp. 485, 488).

But each of them shut up the mind of the Church
to indirect Bible-study. Behind all these stood the
Bible. But it stood behind them, and could not be
got at save through them. Bible-study was, in the
main, secondary. The Fathers were believed to constitute a harmonious body of teaching, so that when
Abelard suggested the contrary, the rulers of the
Church uttered a horrified "Hush!"[1] The Papal
Bulls assumed that the Bullarium was a luminous
exposition of Holy Writ. When Churchmen spoke
about the councils, they assumed that all things they
counted dear could be found within the scope of Vincent's "Believed always, everywhere, and by everybody." And when the three appeals joined their
voices in unison, they made it practically impossible
for the Bible's own voice to be heard, save in so far
as it was in agreement with them.

*Ecclesiasti-
cal infalli-
bility made
Bible-study
secondary.*

Boniface the Eighth, under the stress of opposition
to the rising power of the French monarchy, carried
the statements of the Papacy, if not its claims, higher
than any of his predecessors. Amongst other towering words of his are these, "The Roman Pontifex
has all laws within his breast."[2] If he spoke like a
madman, then his madness was logical. Sometimes it
takes a madman to draw a straight conclusion from a
simple premise. Men in their senses are aware of the
limitations of life, of the need of moderate statement,
of the inevitableness of compromise. A man of great
ability, just a trifle unbalanced, is more fearlessly
logical. Boniface was thoroughly logical. If the
doctrine of papal supremacy is to be seriously taken,

*Boniface
VIII.*

[1] See Bernard's letters.
[2] "Romanus Pontifex, qui jura omnia in scrinio pectoris sui
censetur habere" (In Fr. von Schulte, *Gesch. d. Quellen u.
Literatur d. canon. Rechts von Gratian bis auf die Gegenwart*,
II, p. 34, n. 3).

he was well within his rights.   And in asserting that
the Pope's breast was the place of composition, or

The Papacy the ultimate interpreter. record, for all laws, he asserted, in effect, that the
Popes were the ultimate interpreters of Scripture.   Of
course, neither he nor any other Pope ever proposed
to dispense with the counsel and consent of the
Church at large.   But in him the life and authority
of the Church is centred.   In him the claim of Tradition to be a sufficient interpreter of Scripture is
embodied.   Only through the Papacy, and through
the opinion of the Church as represented in the
Papacy, may the laity hope to get at the right meaning of the Bible.   Now, by reason of the vast vested
interests of the most imposing institution history
has ever seen, the chances of the papal hierarchy
changing its line of interpretation were exceedingly
small.

So long, then, as Bible-study remained under the
control of the papal hierarchy, there could be no direct
approach to the Word of God.   The authority of the
Church jealously guarded the frontiers of all sacred
things.[1]   Inside the frontier the scientific reason had
no rights.[2]   Questions regarding the Bible could not

[1] A sort of intellectual concordat was agreed upon, more
or less unconsciously (Erdmann, *Hist. of Philosophy*, § 216 ;
Ueberweg, *Hist. of Philosophy* (*Ancient and Mediæval*), §§ 102,
104).   Rashdall says truly concerning the great university
movement of the twelfth and thirteenth centuries, that the
"intellectual enthusiasm" of Europe began to flow in a channel separate from religious enthusiasm (*Universities*, I, pp. 29,
30).   But thanks to the concordat whereby reason was relegated
to a sphere of its own, apart from the field of theology and
sacred things, the "humanities" could not touch the text of
Scripture.

[2] Maywald, *Die Lehre von der Zweifacher Wahrheit*, 1871.
The theory of a twofold truth was officially condemned.   For
all that, it was deeply related to the mediæval view of things.

get over the ecclesiastical guard and strike home. Biblical
questions
could not
be pushed
home.
There could be no direct Bible-study.[1] Therefore, a
breach with ecclesiastical Tradition was necessary.
God's Word must go forth from bondage to human
opinion. The Bible refuses to accept the Pope as its
authoritative interpreter. It insists upon interpreting
itself.

The main forces of European life in the sixteenth
century favoured a breach between the Scriptures and
Tradition. The classic age of Tradition, from 500 A.D.
to 1000, was a period of contracting life. But in the
Reformation period life was expanding on every side.
The cry, "Land! Land!" from the masthead of Columbus's ship foretold a new age of commerce and travel,
of widening adventure, of multiplying human interests.[2] "For the inhabitants of Europe, the fourteenth

---

[1] It has been commonly said that the action of Trent in canonising the Vulgate was a mortal blow to sound Bible-study.
E.g. Westcott, *Bible in the Church*, p. 259. This is overdone.
No institution so vast as the Roman Catholic Church ever seriously troubles itself to be consistent. It is no single conciliary
action that affects the course of Bible-study in the Roman
Catholic communion ; rather is it the whole mental attitude
which results from taking the dogma of ecclesiastical infallibility with seriousness and applying it effectively. The dogma
of infallibility, so long as it is an intellectual plaything, may not
permanently retard sound Bible-study. But, vested in a vast
and highly organised hierarchy, it renders thorough and resolute criticism impossible.

[2] The travels of the thirteenth century (Yule, *Marco Polo;*
also, *Cathay and the Way Thither*). Expansion of geographi-
cal knowledge (Fiske, *Old Virginia*, I, pp. 41–43). The study
and theories of Roger Bacon. The body of " earth-knowledge"
began to grow rapidly. Dowden's *Mind and Art of Shakespeare*
gives a brilliant sketch of the mental consequences in the sixteenth century (the Introduction). Hakluyt's *Voyages*, read
in comparison with Butler's *Lives of the Saints*, is a vivid illustration of the new motive and stimulus of life.

The expand-
ing life of the
sixteenth
century.

century had doubled the works of creation." [1]   New
things pressed forward to claim attention.   The
sphere of intelligence was vastly enlarged.   "Never
has a discovery, in itself purely material, produced,
by widening the horizon, a moral change more extraordinary and more durable." [2]   Peter Martyr, writing
in 1493, said, "I feel myself blessed when I speak
with certain sensible men from the number of those
returning from that province" (Hispaniola).   His
friend, Pomponius Lætus, wept for joy when he got
the news. [3]   That letter indicates a vital change in the
centre of mental gravity.   The pleasures of reason
had been found, for many centuries, in the scholastic
philosophy and in the study of the Scriptures under
the tuition of the Fathers.   But now a new world was
coming above the horizon.   And a thrill of joy ran
through men as they thought of the unknown things
that were pressing upon knowledge.

Travellers
take the
place of
pilgrims.

The chief end of the pilgrims, the men who did
the disinterested travelling of Europe for six centuries, was to visit the traditional holy places and to see
as large a number of the bones of the saints as possible. [4]   And they always saw what they went to see.
They did not seek enlargement of knowledge, and they
carried home a minimum acquaintance with new facts.
But with the thirteenth century a new fashion in travel
set in.   And after the fifteenth century the men who
took long journeys, for objects larger than gain, went
to see the new lands, the new things.   The desire to
enlarge the knowledge of Europe led them on.   The
age of Tradition had passed.   The age of mental
curiosity had come.

[1] Humboldt, *Geographie du Nouveau Continent*, 1836, I, viii;
also, *Cosmos* (ed. Bohn), II, 601.
[2] *Ib.*, ix.   [3] *Ib.*, pp. 4, 5.
[4] Beazeley, *The Dawn of Modern Geography*, 1897, ch. 2, 3, 4.

In the nineteenth century men put upon Herschel's tomb the words, "He broke through the barriers of the heavens and added a universe to our knowledge."[1] This is the signature of the period that began in the fifteenth century, — the discovery of the universe; boundless expanses of potential experience encompass the mind. Such an age is necessarily a critical age. For criticism is not an extraordinary form of mental action. The critical reason of our time is identical, in its main qualities, with the scholastic reason of the Middle Ages. The reason is one and the same. It is the circumstances that differ. In the earlier period, the knowledge of facts was nearly at a stand-still. The increments of knowledge came almost wholly from commenting on text-books and from the masterly use of the power of mental abstraction.[2] New facts did not mass themselves on the frontiers of the traditional conceptions. That, however, is what continually happens in our own period. And the result is criticism. Using terms broadly, we may say that the controlling thought of our time is critical.

The explanation is, that vast bodies of new facts have risen behind the old hypotheses and interpretations, assailing them in the rear. In a time of rapidly expanding knowledge, the certainty that truth, unexplored, yet real, stretches out on all sides of the mind, causes a shadow of suspicion to fall upon every

New facts press upon the old hypotheses.

[1] Perrupit claustra, Humboldt, *Cosmos*, I, p. 71.

[2] Whewell, *Hist. of the Inductive Sciences*, 3d ed., 1875, Bk. IV, ch. 2 ("The Commentatorial Spirit"). The mind was content with "collections of opinions," *ib.*, II, p. 187. A similar disposition prevailed in Bible-study. The commentaries were for the most part catenæ, collections of patristic opinions. This tendency began as early as Jerome (Harnack, *Altchrist. Lit.*, *L.*). Direct study, observation, was not the order of the day.

hypothesis.   Reason as a whole becomes critical, constantly challenging the old definitions in the interest of material which they did not include, steadily pressing forward through the old conceptions to unmeasured realities that lie behind them.   Criticism is the mental climate of such a period.

In the sixteenth century the influence of the State was rapidly rising.   Two hundred years before, Philip of France said to Boniface, "Holy Mother Church, the Bride of Christ, is made up not only of clergy, but of laity."[1]   Since then the credit of the secular power had steadily increased.   A hundred years later a great cardinal, Richelieu, allied himself with Protestants in order to exalt France.   The principle of nationality shattered mediæval unity.   It had that result even in literature; for in the fifteenth and sixteenth centuries, the culture of Europe throwing off the common forms that made mediæval literatures, wherever written, so strikingly alike, commenced to nationalise itself.[2]   The records of the printing-press show a steady decline in the number of books written in Latin, a corresponding increase in the number of those written in the modern languages.[3]

Principle of nationality.

The unity of the Canon Law was broken, its domain curtailed.   In the thirteenth and fourteenth centuries it had succeeded in completely emancipating itself from the civil law, and had established an exclusive control over all matters relating to marriages and wills.[4]   But the civil and the common law, strength-

---

[1] Gieseler, *Ecclesiastical History*, Philadelphia, 1836, II, p. 238.

[2] Brunetière, *Hist. d. l. Lit. Française*, 1898, Livre 2, ch. 2.

[3] Paulsen, *Geschichte d. gelehrten Unterrichts*, 1885, Beilage 1. The records of the press in other countries would no doubt give results similar to those in Germany.

[4] Schulte, *Canon Recht*, II, pp. 25–28.

ening with the use of the secular power, kept gaining ground until the sixteenth century, and then its victory was assured. As in literature, so in law, the period of national development had opened. The age of imperial unity in spiritual things was over. The prestige of Tradition had received a mortal wound. Age of imperial unity gone by.

The age of criticism, as we know it, did not come straightway. But the promise of criticism was given when once the break between the Bible and Tradition had been made. For Tradition and criticism are diverse forms of Biblical interpretation. Tradition is the interpretation that sets up the opinions about the Scriptures held by the papal hierarchy as sufficient and authoritative. Criticism is the interpetation that insists upon going behind the interpretation, to put direct questions to the Sacred Books. As soon, then, as the principle of Tradition fell into discredit, the critical principle was conceived. Centuries might pass before it came clearly to the light. None the less, the moment the Bible began to shake off the hold of Tradition, criticism, as a new form of the Church's mental obligation, had won its footing. Fall of Tradition made criticism inevitable.

The obligation of criticism is composed of two elements, the element of conscience and the element of reason. Men are so made that, in the long run, only the best is good in their eyes. If the Bible is the best thing the Church owns, then it is an act of conscience to bring the Bible forth from behind Tradition into direct and quickening touch with the common life of men. Again, if conscience insists upon a first-hand knowledge of God's Word for the sake of the man who needs to be saved, reason insists upon the same thing for the sake of the object to be known. For to every object, great and small, the scientific mind guarantees the right to be seen as it is.

Reformation
an act of
conscience.

The act of conscience made the Reformation.[1] That is not saying that the forces which made the Reformation possible were altogether pure and spiritual. No great historical movement will stand the test of the Sermon on the Mount. When the Children of Israel went up out of Egypt, a mixed multitude went with them. So, when the desire for the pure Word of God carried the Bible outside the bounds of ecclesiastical Tradition, a mixed multitude of desires and motives went along. For all that, the main reason for the movement was the longing of men to see the oracles of God in their original meanings.[2]

Christ and
the Scrip-
tures.

Conscience is the pledge and guarantee of our right to the best. Now the fortunes of Christianity as a historical religion are wrapped up with the fortunes of Christ's book. It is true, of course, that our Lord is not imprisoned within his book. He is the living Head of a living Church, and touches men through the sacraments, the ministry, and the manifold manifestations of his real presence. Yet it is no less true that Christianity without the Bible would be a religion adrift upon the tide of human feeling. Christ's book is God's record of the true process of revelation. It is, therefore, the abiding standard whereby we shall test the spirit that seeks to rule the Church in God's name, so that we may learn whether it is God's Spirit or only the spirit of a period or a time. The Bible, so far as human thought can go, is God's best thing. It is the thing that Christians most deeply need to know.

So it was an act of conscience to appeal to the Bible

[1] Schenkel, *Das Wesen d. Protestantismus*, 1862, §§ 12–30. "The Roman Catholic depotentiation of the Bible."

[2] The connection between the political and the religious elements is admirably wrought out by Ranke, *Hist. of Germany in Period of Reformation*, I.

as the Reformers did. Papal Tradition interposed itself between the religious consciousness and Scripture, asserting that the papal interpretation was the true and sufficient one, and that whosoever sought entry into the Scriptures by any other way was a thief and a robber. But this position no longer satisfied the mature religious sense of Christendom. The Bible is God's best thing for our thought. It must be known as it is in itself. And since Tradition refused to permit men to go behind it, in order to compare it with the Word of God, there was nothing to be done but discard Tradition altogether, in order to achieve a direct study of the Scriptures. *First-hand knowledge of Scripture demanded.*

At the cry, "The Bible and the Bible alone the religion of Protestants,"[1] confusion broke in upon Bible-study. The immediate result was that individual infallibility threatened to take the place of ecclesiastical infallibility. A chaos of conflicting interpretations followed. Historical interpretation was very slow in coming. Even Erasmus, lover of Greek and ardent believer in the human aspects of the New Testament, could contend for the manifold sense of Scripture. Colet, arguing against him, "set down" the manifold meanings found in the texts "not to the fecundity of the Scriptures, but to the sterility of men's minds and their incapacity of getting at the pure and simple truth. If they could but reach that, they would as completely agree as now they differ."[2] This is the ground taken by the exegesis of our time, and, what is more, it is successfully defended against *Historical interpretation came slowly.*

[1] William Chillingworth, *Religion of Protestants*, 1635. He contended for the rational interpretation of Scripture. The clergyman who read the burial service over Chillingworth's body threw the book into his grave, crying, " Go, rot with thine author."

[2] In Seebohm, *The Oxford Reformers* (3d ed.), p. 124.

the assaults of ecclesiastical and dogmatic interests. But it was ground far in advance of the capacities of the age. Other reformers approved of Colet's position.[1] Even three or four swallows, however, do not make a summer. Tradition had held the allegorical interpretation with bit and bridle. Tradition having lost control, and the grammatical-historical interpretation being still in the future, the text continued to lie at the mercy of the interpreter. The difference was that the Pope by the Tiber had given place to the pope in the individual Christian's breast.

Individual infallibility a poor substitute for papal infallibility.

Moreover, Chillingworth's position entailed an unnatural and morbid relationship between the idea of the Church and the idea of the Bible. Rightly understood, these two ideas must live together, if they would live nobly. But the Reformation was necessary. The supreme need of conscience was a true understanding of Scripture. And this could not be hoped for, so long as ecclesiastical opinion claimed infallibility. No matter, then, whether chaos broke loose or not, the Bible must be set up, for the time being, as if it were a thing in itself, apart from the Church's life.

The genius of Christianity required that the book of Life should be opened and that the issues of Church government should be fearlessly examined. Luther wrote to the German nobility, "Hath not the Pope erred? . . . freshly would we judge everything according to Scripture."[2] No longer should the Bible be studied at second hand. The Fathers, looked up to by the Middle Ages as authoritative interpreters, were driven out of their place. "For articles of faith may not be drawn from the words and deeds of the

Luther's words to the German nobility.

---

[1] Luther and Calvin (Farrar, *Interpretation*, pp. 327, 345).
[2] *Primary Works* (Wace and Buchheim).

Fathers. . . . Our creed is that the Word of God alone can ground articles of faith, no one else, not even an angel." [1]

"It is not true," said Petrus Verruilius, "that the Scriptures take their authority from the Church. Their certitude is derived from God and not from men. The Word came before the Church. It is from the Word that the Church holds its vocation." [2] This was a thoroughly representative saying. The Reformers conceived the Church as existing to interpret the Scriptures truly and to bring God's saving Word close to the consciences of men. And if the Church fails to do this, she misses her vocation. But if the authority of the Church must freshly verify itself by the interpretation of the Scriptures, her authority ceases to be for the laity an ultimate thing, and becomes a medium through which the layman is brought into touch with the ultimate. Then, in the last analysis, it is not the authority of the Church that verifies Scripture, but it is Scripture that verifies itself. The Bible is set up as its own interpreter.

The Church must verify herself by the study of Scripture.

While, therefore, at first, the cashiering of Tradition might appear to throw interpretation into confusion by making each individual, however ignorant, a master of interpretation, it was only in appearance. In reality, to set up the Bible as its own interpreter meant, in the long run, that Scripture must be grammatically and historically interpreted. For, on the one side, to throw down the bulwark of Tradition, and invite the common feeling of Christians to test God's Word by direct study, presupposes an entire confidence in the ability of the Bible to take care of itself. The Bible is its own keeper. The Scriptures

---

[1] Smal. Art. To same effect the various Protestant confessions. See Schaff, *Creeds of Christendom.*

[2] In Reuss, *Hist. of the Canon*, p. 296.

F

do not fear what men may do unto them. So Bible-study should be fearless and free. On the other side, the Scriptures, having once asserted the power of self-interpretation, having cast off the guardianship of Tradition, must be studied until they are known in their original sense. And this necessity was sure, in course of time, to usher in the grammatical and historical interpretation.

So the Sacred Books of Christendom were to build up for themselves a defence against chaotic and unworthy renderings. Taken in their own mind and meaning, they can have, as Colet affirmed, only a single sense. This single sense is the safeguard against exegetical abuse — a far better defence than Tradition could provide. For Tradition gained uniformity of interpretation by imposing the allegorical system upon Scripture, along with the proviso that allegory must keep within the bounds marked out by authority. But the tiger does not change his spots when he is put within a cage. The allegorical principle, whether rioting with the Gnostics or forced by the mediæval Church to keep the peace, could have but one upshot. The Scriptures could not be clearly known in their own sense. The best, then, that Tradition could do was to limit the scope of allegorical exegesis. But the Reformation principle, consistently applied, overcame it altogether.

When the Bible came forth from behind Tradition, it sought translation into the people's tongue. The Reformation, being an act of conscience, required that the supreme law of the Church should be published in the language of the laity. Just as the publication of the Twelve Tables at Rome, in the fifth century B.C., indicated that the law of Rome was to be no longer the monopoly of the patricians, so did the widespread enthusiasm for translations of the Bible indicate that

The single sense.

The rights of the laity.

the interpretation of Scripture was to be no longer a monopoly of the priesthood.[1]

This accords well with the nature of Revelation. Our Sacred Books were written by men of the people. They were written for the people. The Bible, by abolishing all distinction between religious truth as it is for the multitude, and the same truth as it is for the religious specialist, makes of itself the most democratic book in the world. It was not possible, then, for the Scriptures to be deeply taken in their own sense so long as a monasticised priesthood held the power of the keys. Written as they were in the broad day of history, enshrining as they do the divine ideals for humanity at large, they must be carried back into the midst of the common life through which their inspiration came, in order to be truly interpreted. So the assertion, by means of translation into the vernacular, of the laity's right to a first-hand knowledge of the Bible was, in effect, an assertion of the Bible's right to be understood.

The Bible taken back to the common life.

The religious motive at work in the movement of the sixteenth century effected a breach between Bible-study and Tradition. It did this because the essence of religion is the desire to be saved; that is, the desire to be in close and cleansing touch with the ultimate realities of life. The Bible, as God's book of Witness to the fundamental qualities and final issues of life, required to be known at first-hand, if men were to be truly saved. So conscience cashiered Tradition. At the same time, the downfall of Tradition, of the sacerdotal monopoly of interpretation, threw the doors of Bible-reading and Bible-study wide open to the laity. While the breach with Tradition involved the direct study of Scripture, the incoming

The Bible-study of the laity.

[1] Moulton, *Hist. of the English Bible*, pp. 21, 22.

of the laity involved free study.   For the lay mind of Europe must needs move with the lay will; and the lay will, building up the modern State, could not stop short of orderly freedom, political and mental.[1] When Christianity established itself in the Roman Empire, the Bible became the Vade-mecum, the book of devotion, for Europe.   When, in the sixteenth century, Tradition's claim to be an authoritative interpretation was rejected, the Bible entered into the expanding life of the Occident.   Henceforth it must take its chances in a climate of free action and free thought.[2]

The religious motive of Bible-study not sufficient.

Thus, through the religious motive, the first great step was taken in the direction of criticism.   The original thought and feeling of Scripture must be discovered and appropriated.   Once started upon this road, where could Bible-study bring up, short of the historical interpretation?

But the religious motive, by itself, would not have been equal to the work of discovering and shaping these new principles of interpretation which the nature of revelation called for.   The Bible, in its essence, is a history, a body of facts; its saving thought is intelligible only in connection with those facts.   As a history, and, what is more, a history moving over a very broad field of time, it needs to be studied in the light of history at large.   Now, work of that sort is the function of reason.   For reason exists to see things as they are.   As Bacon finely said, it "doth buckle and bow the mind unto the nature of things."

[1] Ranke calls the Reformation period one of the "greatest conjunctions" of universal history, I, p. 243.

[2] This stands out very clearly in the history of England and America.   The Bible has been knit up into the life of free peoples.   The free mental action that accompanies free life must touch the Bible to the quick.   The Bible must submit to the most searching examination or cease to be our national book.

The religious motives of the Reformation, the splendid protest of conscience against vicars and substitutes for realities, laid upon the Church the obligation to return to the first sources of our religion. Reason alone, however, — scientific curiosity, multiplying the materials of knowledge and shaping its methods, — could create the apparatus of historical Bible-study.

In the thirteenth century, the mediæval Church had made a concordat with reason. The field of experience was divided. There were to be two bodies of truth, and they were not to harass each other. On the frontier between them stood the infallible authority and Tradition of the Church. Behind Tradition the Scriptures lay secure, beyond the reach of such questions as an impassioned love of truth always forces home. Raymond of Sabonde, in his *Natural Theology* published about 1436, put the point perfectly when he said that there are two books, the book of Nature and the book of Scripture; and that the former is open to everybody, while the latter is only open to the priesthood.[1] So reason could not get at the sacred text save through authority. That meant that reason, when it crossed the frontier between the study of Nature and the study of Scripture, surrendered its sword. The Bible was secure.

The concordat of the thirteenth century.

The security was dearly bought. We must again remind ourselves that an authority of the mediæval sort could not be efficiently worked, unless by a monasticised Church headed up in a Pope. So the Bible, fleeing from reason to find asylum in authority, must be content when the deepest elements in its own nature are suppressed or kept in the background. The heart of Scripture is its view of the creative, saving unity of the divine life as revealed through a human expe-

Price paid by Scripture for insurance against questions.

[1] Hagenbach, *Dogmengesch.*, § 159.

rience worked out under historical conditions. If the
Bible, then, in order to be unvexed by reason, takes
the veil and becomes the text-book of a monasticised
Church, it allows its own fundamental qualities to be
overshadowed.

The Bible would not pay the price. If, as the book
of Witness to God's best things, it demanded a direct
touch on the lay conscience, as a book of history it
demanded, with equal insistence, a direct touch on
the lay reason.

In the movement called the Renaissance, the reason
of Europe began to claim again the right of suffrage
in things spiritual. It had gone into bankruptcy in
the fifth century, when the State broke down. For
many centuries thereafter, all the truth that seemed
vital to man passed into the keeping of men living the
monastic life and separated, as far as possible, from
the conditions under which the layman lives and
within which his reason works. But the principle
of the Renaissance was the exaltation of lay learning,
— the learning of the Greeks and the Romans. To be
sure, the Latin classics had been read all through the
Middle Ages. Not, however, in and for themselves.
Rather as forerunners of Christianity. The Renaissance made them an end in themselves. The difference is profound.[1]   In the one case they were treated
as if they stood within the mediæval view of life. In
the other case, they called the mind away from that
view. This involved a revolution in the aims and
methods of education. The mediæval universities
were, in the main, clerical establishments.[2] The
teaching staff was made up almost wholly of men in

Growing
self-confi-
dence of
reason.

[1] Brunetière, *Lit. Franç.*, pp. 41, 42.

[2] Rashdall, *Universities;* Denifle, *Entstehung d. Universitä-
ten des Mittelalters*, 1885. The words of the text need to be
qualified, but they are substantially sound.

orders or men under the monastic vows. They were within the sphere and under the discipline of the Papacy. Vital truth, all the truth that touched the heart and quickened the imagination, was controlled by Tradition. But the Renaissance brought the mind of the Occident to a sharp turn in the road. It brought to light new principles of education. It contained the promise of a new type of university. It exalted lay learning. It involved the emancipation of reason from authority.

Revolution in education.

Ultimately, Tradition must justify itself before reason, even as the Reformation forced it to justify itself before conscience. Hooker, the great Englishman, wrote, " Although ten thousand general councils would set down one and the same definitive sentence concerning any point of religion whatsoever, yet one demonstrative reason alleged or one manifest testimony cited from the mouth of God himself to the contrary, could not choose but overweigh them all." [1] In words like these the relationship between the two elements in the sixteenth-century movement comes out. The desire to know and the desire to be saved must work together in order to settle the accounts between Revelation and Tradition. The Bible freely puts itself within the reach of reason.

Tradition and reason.

The Reformation and the Renaissance created a resistless demand for the original text of the Scripture. The mediæval Church, fixing the lines of her character in the counter-Reformation, blundered into an undue valuation of the Vulgate. But Protestantism went straight to the Greek and the Hebrew. And the free study of the times travelled the same road. How closely the needs of awakening reason and the needs of the quickened conscience kept together may

Demand for the original texts.

[1] Hooker, *Ecclesiastical Polity*, II, 5, 7.

be seen in the work of Reuchlin, who published the first Hebrew grammar, in 1506,[1] and of Erasmus, who put out the first Greek Testament, in 1516. Erasmus urged the need of improved texts of the Fathers. Reuchlin proclaimed the necessity of the original text of Aristotle. Men had outgrown the secondary sources of knowledge that satisfied the Middle Ages.[2]

With well-nigh incredible heat men laid hold of the rudiments of Greek and Hebrew. The study of grammar became a matter of prime importance. In effect this meant the downfall of the allegorical method of interpretation which had reigned, without a break, since the second century. The simple, historical sense of Scripture became, in principle, the final and decisive sense. And therewith the human authors of our Sacred Books were restored to honour. For allegory, when it exalted the mystical and theological meanings of Scripture far above the historical, by one and the self-same mental act, so conceived the divine that in its presence the human lost colour and individuality.

Protestantism was inconsistent. The principles of

[1] Reuchlin was fully self-conscious regarding the significance of his work. " Exegi monumentum ære perennius," he wrote.

[2] The entire scholarly movement of the sixteenth century was toward the direct study of the ancients. It constituted a veritable revolution of reason. One might find a good illustration of the " critical " bias, the bent toward direct study of antiquity, in the history of Egyptology. The first feeble attacks upon the hieroglyphs were made between 1529 and 1589. Kept up through the seventeenth and eighteenth centuries, it was not until 1799 that the Rosetta stone was found, which a few years later gave to Champollion the *entrée* into Egyptian antiquity. Ed. Meyer, *Gesch. d. alten Aegyptens*, 1887 ; *Einleitung*, pp. 282–313. The dates synchronise with the course of the Higher Criticism closely enough to be instructive,

the Reformation were not followed home. The doctrine of ecclesiastical infallibility was thrown overboard. But the cognate doctrine of Scriptural infallibility was retained and even exaggerated. In the Middle Ages the two doctrines grew together. The idea of the Bible and the idea of the Church were practically identified. In the sixteenth century the two ideas parted company. The Roman wing of Christianity proceeded to force and strain the idea of the Church. The Protestant wing, for a time, forced and strained the idea of inspiration. It even came to pass, in the seventeenth century, that the Roman Catholic scholars held far more liberal views of inspiration than the Protestants.[1]

As a temporary thing this inconsistency might be pardoned. Under the circumstances it was entirely natural. The case is parallel to the prodigious emphasis that the sixteenth and seventeenth centuries put upon the divine right of kings. In those days the Monarchy was the Protestant bulwark against the Papacy. It was well-nigh inevitable that political theory should make much of the divine right of kings.[2] Even so, the infallibility of the Bible was set up as a bulwark against the infallibility of the Church. Naturally the theory of literal inspiration was strained to the uttermost.[3] Natural as it was, however, it was none the less a dire inconsistency. The Protestant principle brought forward the human authors of Scripture and insured their standing with the Divine Author. The Protestant practice drove them out of His presence. So the Reformation went

Protestant-
ism not
consistent.

[1] Hagenbach, *Dogmengeschichte*, § 243.

[2] Maine, *Ancient Law* (3d Am. ed.), p. 334.

[3] The claim of inspiration even for the Hebrew vowel-points shows how the theory was strained until it snapped (Diestel, § 39).

limping and halting.   The sacred text still lay at the mercy of allegory.[1]

The promise of historical interpretation given.   In spite, however, of backsets and hindrances, the pledge and assurance of a human, historical interpretation of Scripture had been given.   Once given, it could not be recalled.   A mighty clerical establishment like the Roman Catholic Church can put off for an indefinite period the frank and full discussion of the ultimate question touching the nature and scope of revelation.   But the Protestant churches could not long postpone it.   Once and for all they had rejected the sacerdotal monopoly of interpretation.   Once and for all the Bible had gone forth into the open field of free life and thought.   After the third century the *forum publicum* of the Church, the body of men who put questions and gave answers about sacred things, was made up mainly, at times almost wholly, of the clergy.   The laity now pressed in to claim a place on the jury.[2]

Bible-reading.   The Bible became the people's Bible, and Bible-reading a widespread habit.[3]   The habit had no great spread in the ancient Church.   In the latter Middle

[1] Thus Tradition successfully reasserted itself as a sufficient and practically final interpretation of the sacred text (Gründberg, *Spener*, 1892, pp. 23, 24).

[2] Speaking broadly, there are four periods in the history of the *forum publicum* for theological, that is to say, primary questions.   (1) In the conciliar action of the Nicene period, the laity have no direct part, save in so far as they were represented by the Emperor.   (2) The bishops get complete control of the clergy.   This carries the primary question farther away from the laity.   (3) The Pope conquers the episcopate.   This takes the primary question still farther away from the judgments and criticisms of the lay world.   (4) The rise of the laity since the sixteenth century.

[3] " Bibel-Lesung " in *Realencyclopädie* (3e Auf.) ; Reuss, *Hist. of the N. T.*, §§ 424, 458, 459, 465, 468, 500.

Ages, it gained ground. That is proved by the attitude of the hierarchy in and after the thirteenth century. In the fifteenth century, popular appreciation of the Bible grew strong. That is shown by the considerable number of translations. Just at this time the printing-press came to the help of God's Word. We have here a very striking illustration of the way in which the spiritual and the mechanical elements of history work together. In the patristic period a man could not carry about with him the entire Bible. The shape and bulk of books in those days rendered it impossible. But the form of the modern Bible had been reached before the printing-press came into use. Thus, when the hour struck for the passing of the Scripture out of the control of the clergy, the mechanical agencies of civilisation were on hand to do their full part.[1]

The laity began to be Bible-students.[2] The story of Bradford, the first governor of Plymouth Colony, is a vivid proof that the change brought about by the Reformation was a mighty one. In his old age, this heroic Pilgrim, who had done a man's full work in the rough New World, took up the study of Hebrew. He desired "to see with his own eyes the ancient oracles of God in all their pristine beauty." What a change since the days of Jerome! A layman, a pioneer, his hands hardened by the sword and roughened by the axe, studying Hebrew in his old age! A revolutionary departure this from the state of things prevailing in the Middle Ages. Then no man might see the Scriptures save through the medium of the

Story of Bradford.

[1] Stevens well says that "the secular history of the Holy Scriptures is the sacred history of printing" (*Bible in the Caxton Exhibition*, 1877, p. 25).

[2] Cassiodorus in the sixth century was a Bible-student after a fashion. But he went to the monastery to get his Bible-class.

Fathers.   But now the Bible is its own interpreter. And it is face to face with the layman's world, the new world of the spirit.   No longer can there be two bodies of truth that come not near each other.   All truth must be vitally related.   Once and for all the Bible abandons the cloisters of mediæval Tradition, where security is paid for by misinterpretation.   Once and for all the Scriptures pass out into the world where philosophy and science claim a divine right to be, and where the layman, looking into his heart, speaks his mind freely.

CHAPTER V

THE CRITICAL PRINCIPLE WINS ITS FOOTING[1]

IT was in the eighteenth century that criticism became an historical force. The mental conditions of the time differed profoundly from those of the early Middle Ages. If the latter was the classic age of Tradition, then the eighteenth century was the classic age of scepticism touching Tradition. The typical reasoner in the first case was a man who looked at the Scriptures through the interpretation of the Fathers, and who looked at the universe through such fragments of ancient knowledge as had come down to him. Authority was the first word of the mediæval man. It was also his last. For when, in the fourteenth century, Occam gave up Anselm's attempt to make Tradition seem rational, he did not, for that reason, give up faith. Things might be true in theology that were false in philosophy, and contrariwise. For all that, the devout son of the Church held fast his belief and bowed to the authority of the Church.

The typical man of the eighteenth century threw

The eighteenth century.

---

[1] Literature : Paulsen, *German Universities*, tr. 1895, *Geschichte d. gelehrten Unterrichts*, 1885 ; Lecky, *Hist. of Rationalism ;* Hettner, *Literaturgeschichte d. achtzehnten Jahrhunderts*, 1872 ; Morley, *Voltaire, Rousseau, Diderot ;* Leslie Stephen, *English Thought in the Eighteenth Century.* The justification and necessity of these general references is found in the fact that the eighteenth century is the decisive turn of our history. To understand its mental character is a fundamental need.

Character-
istics.

Tradition upon the dust-heap.   He cared nothing for
the Fathers.   He did not care much for books.   Descartes' scorn of book-learning was representative.
His resolve to know his own mind thoroughly was
prophetic.[1]   Bacon, however he might differ from Descartes in matters of method, was not a whit more
modern than he.   The two together were the heralds
of the new age of mental life.   All intellectual
"idols," all the notions that came down out of the
past, with the mark of Aristotle and the schoolmen
on them, were to be turned out of doors.   No traditions, scholastic or ecclesiastical, shall thrust themselves between reason and reality.   All knowledge
shall be first-hand.

Individual-
ism.

The eighteenth-century man fully possessed himself.   He cried down the ancients and cried up the
moderns.[2]   No kind of experience, though ever so
true in its time and place, could set itself up as a
classic.   He built upon his own reason and intuitions.
In the strongest sense he was an individual.   The
mediæval man had lived and thought as a member of
a corporation, or a class, or a Church; he had a deep,
naïve faith in all the traditions, whether sacred or
secular.[3]   But the eighteenth-century man thought

[1] Contrast with the "commentatorial method" of the Middle
Ages.   Descartes' *Treatise on Method* was, to use a much-
abused phrase, epoch-making (Huxley's essay on Descartes in
Lay Sermons).

[2] Bacon's adage, "Antiquitas sæculi juventus mundi," indicated antiquity's loss of prestige.   Rigault, *Le querelle des
anciens et des modernes*, 1856 ; Flint, *Philosophy of History*
("France "), 1894, pp. 212–215.

[3] If the student should glance at Thomas Stanley's *Hist. of
Philosophy* (1st ed., London, 1655), and contrast it with any
modern history of philosophy, he would quickly see that the
faith of the mediæval and early modern world in ancient traditions was sweeping.   It was quite as childlike in dealing with

for himself, — or thought that he did; and that, for our purpose, amounts to the same thing. He shook off not one kind of tradition, but all kinds. Hume declared that the first page of Thucydides was the commencement of real history.[1] Schleiermacher, when a mere boy in his twelfth year, was tortured by the suspicion that all the ancient records, both sacred and profane, might turn out to be forgeries.[2] Historic doubt was widespread.

So it came to pass that the word "antiquity," which, for so many centuries, had been a word of inspiration, even a word to conjure with, now became a word that called up a problem. Ceasing to be an authority, reverenced and exploited, it turned into a body of facts, or possibilities of fact, which must be studied and explored.

It were easy to dwell on the negative side of the historic doubt of the eighteenth century. It were equally easy to dwell on the mediæval saint's indifference to personal cleanliness. But every great tendency must be estimated by the flower it puts forth, not by the muck in which it grows. The mood of mediæval sainthood put forth the Gothic cathedral and the *Imitation*. And the eighteenth century put forth the historical spirit of the nineteenth. Historic doubt made Niebuhr possible.[3]

the traditions regarding the Greek philosophers as in its dealing with the legends of the Apostles. It was a universal bias (Chwolson, *Die Ssabier*, 1856, I, pp. 3, 4).

[1] Essay on the *Populousness of Ancient Nations. Life and Letters of Niebuhr* (tr. by Winkworth), II, p. 433.

[2] *Life* (tr. by Rowan), I, p. 4. "My twelfth year . . . I conceived the idea that all the ancient authors, and with them the whole of ancient history, were supposititious." Cf. Descartes' resolution to begin his mental life by doubting everything.

[3] It is something better than a mere coincidence that the 2d edition of De Beaufort's *Diss. sur l'incertitude des cinq pre-*

Power of
the new
learning.

For the prime mental quality of the eighteenth century man was not his doubts and negations. They were on the surface. Below them was a deep, strong sense of outlying fact, of truth waiting to be known, of a new world of undiscovered, but discoverable things. In this field the story of Anquetil du Perron is as representative and as refreshing as the story of Bayard is in a very different field.[1] He was born in 1731. Studying in Paris he acquainted himself with Hebrew, Arabic, and Persian. He happened upon a fragment of the Zend-Avesta in the Royal Library at Paris. It kindled in him the desire to see India, and to learn the Zend and the Sanscrit languages. To that end, he enlisted as a common soldier, that he might be sent to India, and there find an opening into those regions of knowledge whither no European had penetrated. His life is typical of the eighteenth century in its promise and potency. The consciousness f facts standing outside all existing knowledge and casting suspicion upon the established framework of knowledge, was its chief characteristic.

It was in this century that criticism was born.

---

miers siècles de l'histoire romaine appeared in 1750, nearly synchronous with the beginning of Semler's Bible-work. This reference is taken from Puchta, *Institutionen* (6ᵉ Auf., 1865), I, p. 101, n. Flint, *Phil. of H.*, pp. 253-261. Beaufort's *Dissertation* suggests Niebuhr, although widely different in spirit ; it indicates the fact that the mind of Western Europe had entered a "critical" climate. The first parts of Niebuhr's Roman History issued in 1811–1812. If the term "epoch-making" had not been rendered useless by overuse, we should call it "epoch-making" in the fullest sense. See Stanley's *Life of Arnold* for the profound impression it made.

[1] *Translation of the Avesta*, 1771 ; *Législation Orientale*, 1778. One catches from his work the same thrill of discovery and mental enlargement that we feel in the letters of Columbus. Alfred Cave, *Introduction to Theology* (2d ed.), p. 209.

from the conditions and causes that gave it birth we may draw a definition of its essential nature. The main condition was the bankruptcy of Tradition, leaving the mind free to know and possess itself. The main cause was the sense of outlying facts. So we define criticism as a movement of the human mind, inspired by the consciousness of truth unknown, but knowable, and sustained by the resolution to serve the truth without fear or favour. This definition is indeed a general one, having no specific reference to Bible-study. All the better. It will serve to remind us that the critical period of Bible-study is part and parcel of the general mental movement of Europe. *Criticism born.*

The eighteenth-century man was a Deist. In the place of ecclesiastical infallibility he put his own infallibility. Even if he was too well-bred to speak like Tom Paine, calling theology a mischievous invention of priests and proclaiming his own mind to be his Church, yet, in effect, he constituted a Church of one: his religion found its sole authority in his reason. Moreover, he spoke with authority on theological questions. His dogmas were indeed few and portable. Yet, such as they were, he took them with great seriousness. His confidence in the rightfulness and conclusiveness of his own theological processes was absolute.[1] *Deism.*

Furthermore, — and this is the most significant point, — in a great majority of cases, the leading Deists were laymen.[2] They inaugurated a lay move- *The lay movement in theology.*

[1] Sidney Lee, *Autobiography of Edward, Lord Herbert of Cherbury*, 1886. Herbert of Cherbury, in contrast with Bayard and with the Puritans. He marks the arrival of a new type.

[2] England was the birthplace of Deism, because it was the home of the self-governing layman. It is interesting to note that the first English Deist was a Member of Parliament. See speech of a "Gentleman from Gray's Inn" (1530) in **Rhys**

G

ment in theology.   The bearings of this fact upon the history of criticism are easily found.   If we are careful to distinguish between that mental attitude which is the spring and source of criticism and that body of opinions touching special points and special questions with which it is often confused, we shall define Biblical criticism as the applications of scientific methods to the textual and literary study of our Scriptures. Now, the soul of science is its disposition toward facts as a whole.   And this disposition or mental temperament is a result of a union between two elements. The first is the desire to know facts just as they are, without regard to the vested interests of society. The second is the sense of outlying fact, of things unknown invading the frontiers of knowledge, the sense, too, of unexplored and undiscovered meanings in those things with which, so far as appearances go, the mind may long have been intimate.

Philosophy.   Both the desire to know and the sense of outlying fact are parts of the lay movements of reason.   Of course, that is a somewhat rough and ready statement. But, taking history broadly, it is sufficiently exact to satisfy practical requirements.   The history of philosophy proves this.   The Greeks founded philosophy. And their philosophy was part and parcel of a rich development of lay life; that is, of human life as it unfolds itself along the secular lines of trade and travel and widening experience, of systematised observation, of art and politics.   When Greek philosophy finished its course, theology succeeded it as

Davids, *Hibbert Lectures*, 1882, pp. 5, 6.   The gentleman from Gray's Inn brings forward the discontent of "laiques and secular persons" and seeks the "catholic and common notions" which Herbert of Cherbury knew he had found.   See also Leslie Stephen, *English Thought*, and Hettner, *Literaturgeschichte d. achtzehnten Jahr.*, I.

the highest form of thought. Such, in truth, it by nature is, and such, in the long run, it will show itself to be. But the theology that dominated the Occident from the beginning of the second century to the fourteenth, was a theology produced almost wholly by men in orders. In the Middle Ages, it was well-nigh exclusively the affair of men who had taken the monastic vows. Philosophy, the tradition of lay thought and learning, never lost its continuity. Straight down through the darkest ages it maintained its dignity as an intellectual tradition. But for a long time it was a bare tradition. And even after the great intellectual revival of the twelfth and thirteenth centuries, philosophy was not truly philosophic. For the essence of philosophy is the freedom of its look at the universe. It matters not whether the philosopher be a layman or a man in orders. But it matters a great deal, everything in fact, whether a layman shall have the self-confidence to philosophise, and to philosophise with no man to make him afraid.

Moreover, philosophy contradicts its own nature, if it stops short at some boundary marked out by authority and bows its head to listen to the words, "Thus far and no farther!" The spirit of philosophy is a free look at things and a free look at all things. To permit authority to shut it up to a contemplation of "secular" things, or to put it off with a merely preliminary view of "sacred" things, while the real body of "sacred" things is reserved for the study and contemplation of a clerical hierarchy, were to deny itself.[1] That is precisely what mediæval philosophy did when it made a concordat or compromise with Tradition in the thirteenth century.

Authority of reason.

[1] Ueberweg, *Hist. of Philosophy* (*Ancient and Mediæval*), pp. 355–357, 443.

In truth, mediæval philosophy was not philosophy at all, since philosophy can recognise no authority save the inherent laws of human nature and mind, and since those laws can only authenticate themselves as laws by opening themselves to a free and fearless examination.   Besides, if mediæval philosophy gainsaid the nature of philosophy, mediæval theology no less gainsaid the nature of true theology.   For theology, if it is to be permanently and for all men the highest form of thought, must establish itself within the common sense and reason of mankind. And in order to do that, it must give to the layman the privilege of debate.

It is from this point of view that we see the full significance of Deism.   It was the initiation of the lay movement in theology.   The words are accurate enough for all practical purposes.   The Deist thought himself competent to speak upon all these points which the Tradition of the Middle Ages had reserved to the hierarchy.   Whether he was really competent or not is no concern of ours.   It is his supreme self-confidence that interests us here.   And that, taken in connection with the fact that the common feeling of the eighteenth century fully admitted his competence, is a most momentous matter.   For it published and spread far and wide the belief that the lay reason need not shrink from applying to the most sacred objects the same methods of research and examination which commend themselves as means to a richer and more accurate knowledge of the world at large.

Criticism is not, primarily, any given set of opinions regarding the Bible.   Not a few "critical" opinions are less "critical" than some "traditional" opinions, inasmuch as they are equally haughty and overbearing and, at the same time, are farther from the real facts in the case.   Criticism is not this or that opinion;

Laymen competent to speak on the mysteries.

What is criticism?

neither is it this or that body of opinions. It is an intellectual temperament, a mental disposition. Its premise is the unity of truth; authority shall not draw a line between "sacred" truth and "secular" truth: truth is one. The ideal is the free study of all facts, howsoever named and catalogued. There is, indeed, order and precedence in facts. And there are diverse human faculties at work in the testing and authentication of facts. But access to the whole body of facts must be full and free. The Bible, if it is to be a permanent part of the Occidental layman's world, — the world of political freedom and reverent devotion to truth, — if it will not content itself with being the "Good Book" of weak women, and helpless children, and priests in petticoats, must come within reach of the scientific reason.

The lay movement in theology was partly the result of theological indifference. The fearful religious wars that devastated Europe for more than a hundred years were followed by a kind of glacial epoch in theology. Dogma, apart from the simple system of the Deists, became abhorent. Systematic divinity, long the queen of the sciences, was now a Cinderella.[1]

Theological indifference

[1] Kant, in the Preface to the first edition of the *Critique*, says regarding metaphysics : "Es war eine Zeit, in welcher sie die *Königin* aller Wissenschaften genannt wurde. . . . Jetzt (1781) bringt es der Modeton des Zeitalters so mit sich, ihr alle Verachtung zu beweisen, u. die Matrone klagt, verstossen u. verlassen wie Hecuba : modo maxima rerum, tot generis natisque potens . . . nunc trahor exul, inops." Even more truly might this have been said of theology whose " ancilla," — handmaid, — philosophy had once been glad to be.

The Pope's suppression of the Jesuits is a striking proof that the eighteenth century was the glacial epoch in theology. F. A. Wolff's philological seminar (he died in 1824) is an illustration. He would not permit a theological student to enter it (Arnoldt, *F. A. Wolff*, I, pp. 97, 98). This was not because

In part, the lay movement was the upshot of mental competition. We remember that in the classic period of Tradition mental competition did not exist. The Greek and Roman classics, so far as they were known, were lowly handmaids of the established interpretation of the Scriptures. But with the Renaissance "new things" began to compete with the old. At first the competition was unconscious. Later, entering into consciousness, its possible dangers were detected by the guardians of the established view. The new things being assigned to a definite sphere, the effects of mental competition were checked and controlled. Finally, however, in the eighteenth century, the new things triumphed for a time over the old. "Nature," or the truth and experience lying outside all tradition and lying especially remote from all theological traditions, became supremely, absorbingly interesting. Franklin with his kite attracted more attention than Thomas Aquinas with his *Summa*. Linnæus, with his reform of botanical terminology, was more significant than the most acute dogmatician. Cook, voyaging around the world, was thought to be doing work far more important than theological discussion. The centre of mental gravity had shifted.[1]

New interests competing with the old.

he abhorred theology, but because he wished to separate the teacher's profession from the minister's. But this ousting of the minister from the higher teaching went along with the downfall of theology. Wolff's seminar was of great importance in the mental life of Germany (Arnoldt, I, pp. 79–88; Herman Schiller, *Gesch. d. Pädagogik*, 1891, § 27).

[1] (1) On the side of the more popular movement. The history of modern feeling about Nature (Gribble, *The Early Mountaineers*, 1899 (especially ch. 3); Stopford Brooke, *Theology in the English Poets;* Humboldt, *Cosmos*.

(2) *Hist. of the Novel.* It is an interesting chapter in the history of the mental competition that has changed the face of the Occident. Pattison, speaking of the brilliant success of

But, whatever the causes, the consequence was clear. The entire dogma of infallibility dissolved. For that dogma rested upon authority, upon the ecclesiastical right to reserve certain questions as outside the competence of reason, as above the reach of real questions. Protestantism, after throwing ecclesiastical infallibility overboard, let out the last reef in Biblical infallibility. And with the result that it temporarily dismasted itself. The whole conception of infallibility had to go. Under that condition alone could a critical study of the Scripture become possible. For the dissolution of the belief in infallibility was the negative aspect of the positive work of the eighteenth century, namely, the affirmation of the competence of reason in all things, sacred as well as secular.[1]

Thus, the eighteenth century became a precipitation-point in universal history, one of those rare conjunctions of causes and conditions which lay bare the foundations of life and enable men to ask the ultimate questions. The limitations of the period were marked. It lacked reverence. It starved the imagination. It had no capacity for great poetry. Its fundamental heresy was the belief that the historical and the ideal cannot closely touch, far less penetrate each other.[2] But pronounced limitations are apt to go with great

Dogma of infallibility goes to pieces.

Baronius' history and its subsequent disappearance, says that it appealed to the "hagiographical temper": "the competition of the secular novel, which came in the seventeenth century, tended to throw hagiography into the shade" (*Life of Casanbon*, p. 380).

[1] The dominant word in speculative things was common sense, the standard of truth and use set up in the bosom of the average man.

[2] Kaftan, *Truth of the Christian Religion*, I, pp. 249, 250 ; Windelband, *Hist. of Philosophy*, p. 497 ; Pfleiderer, *The Philosophy of Religion*, I, pp. 102–108 ; Harnack, *Christianity and History* (tr. 1896), pp. 19–23.

virtues. It is so with individuals and nations. It is so with historical periods. The defects of the eighteenth century waited upon its great mental virtue. By its idolatry of common sense and its worship of reason, by the splendid self-reliance it fostered, by its glorification of the right and duty of research into all the outlying facts that touch and challenge human attention, it delivered the Occident from the tyranny of dogma and Tradition. The ground was cleared for historical study.[1]

The term "critical."

The word "critical" now broke loose. It preëmpted all fields of experience. Like the word "evolution" in our own time, it coloured all thought and was even made a substitute for thinking.[2] Like every word that has made a permanent fortune, it indicated a new turn of feeling. In this case the turn was revolutionary. Tradition entailed the acceptance of certain long-established views regarding the Sacred Books. Tradition having broken down, criticism took possession of the mind, calling for a fresh study of all the data

[1] The life and work of Niebuhr is a typical one. His work bore upon the entire field of historical criticism. An English reviewer of the translation of his Roman history bewailed it on the ground that the next thing to be assailed would be the early O. T. history.

[2] The catalogue of any great library, *s.v.* "criticism" and "critical," will show that, with the entrance of the eighteenth century, the word began to run almost like wildfire. The career of a word is sometimes full of instruction. Compare the career of the word "evolution" after the publication of Darwin's *Genesis of Species*. In the Preface to the first edition of the *Critique*, Kant said with truth : "Unser Zeitalter ist das eigentliche Zeitalter der Kritik, der sich alles unterwerfen muss."

The universal critical tendency of the eighteenth century is connected with the movement toward social revolution. See Comte, *Philosophie Positive*, IV (1839), pp. 9–51. His words, while exaggerated, are suggestive.

involved. The old source of knowledge must be made more of, and new sources opened. The true text of experience must be discovered, the original facts laid bare.

The downfall of the doctrine of infallibility threw the Scriptures open to observation. As the old conception of inspiration lost credit, men's eyes were enabled to see the human aspects of the sacred text. A good illustration of this process is found in the history of the "Purist" controversy. The conservative scholars started with the unconscious assumption that the style of the Greek Testament could not be a whit less perfect than the best "classic" Greek. No "barbarism," no slips of construction, no words which, from a literary point of view, were uncouth or awkward, could be found in it. Their opponents contended that, as a matter of fact, the Greek of the New Testament was not "pure," did not conform to the classical standard; that St. Paul did not write as well as Plato. The debate lasted a long time. The conservatives were moved by the highest motives. Yet they were as men whom dogma had blinded to facts. The debate could end in but one way. The style of the New Testament is as perfect for its purpose as any style can possibly be.[1] But its Greek is not classical Greek. And the moment the old conception of inspiration weakened, the facts of the case came into clear view.[2]

Ancient idea of inspiration dissolves.

Scriptural facts can be seen.

The text of Scripture was no longer defended or enslaved by Tradition. Reason was free to do its whole work, bad as well as good.

It was natural that the criticism of the text, the so-called "Lower Criticism," should first take the

[1] Renan, *Les Evangiles*, p. 99.
[2] Bleek, *Introduction to N. T.*, I, pp. 58, 59 ; Bleek-Mangold, *Einleitung in d. N. T.*, p. 13.

field.   The history of Protestantism made this inevitable.   On the one hand, the Reformed churches, setting
the Bible in opposition to the Church, made it necessary to appeal to the original form of Scripture; they
would have no patience with quotations from the Vulgate.   On the other hand, by cashiering the principle of ecclesiastical authority, they brought the text
within reach of observation.   And, at the same time,
by straining the doctrine of inspiration to the break-
ing-point, they rendered themselves morbidly sensi-
tive to any suggestion of uncertainty touching the
original and authentic words of Scripture.

Deists assail
Protestant-
ism.

When the fierce religious wars of the sixteenth and
seventeenth centuries were over, when men sat down
to think in cold blood, Protestantism was exposed to
attack in two directions.   From the rear the Deists
assailed it.   They were free-thinking laymen.   They
first won the right of free speech in Protestant countries, — England, for example.   Devout scholars,
Walton and Mill, had assembled a large number of
variants.   The Deists used these variants to shatter
the current Protestant conception of inspiration.
"All is over," they triumphantly said, "with the traditional views of the Scriptures!"   How great was
the alarm in England, how serious the crisis appeared
to the leading men within the churches, may be seen
in the life of Bentley.[1]   The dangers of the situation
set him to thinking upon the right methods of reaching
through the variants to the original text.

The Roman
Catholic
attack.

The Roman Catholic scholars attacked Protestantism
in front.   They did not strain the doctrine of inspiration.   On the contrary, developing the idea of ecclesiastical infallibility, they were able to adopt more
liberal views.   It served their purpose well to prove

---

[1] R. C. Jebb, *Bentley*, 1882, p. 158.

that the sacred text was not everywhere certain and clear. Thus, Simon said that the variants in the text could be used "to show that the Protestants had no assured principle for their religion."[1] If a great scholar, as Simon undoubtedly was, could thus use the New Testament variants as a weapon against Protestantism, beyond doubt the average Roman Catholic disputant used them freely.

This double attack made Textual Criticism necessary. The life of Bengel makes very real to us the pain and grief inflicted upon noble natures by the fact that the text seemed to be uncertain. Writing in 1725, he says, "More than twenty years ago, before Mill appeared, at the very beginning of my academic life, when I happened upon an Oxford exemplar, I was greatly distressed by the various readings; but all the more was I driven to examine Scripture carefully, so far as my slender abilities would permit, and afterward, by God's grace, I got new strength of heart."[2] Bengel was a man of deep piety. Living in the

The "Lower Criticism."

---

[1] "Pour montier que les Protestans n'avoient aucun principe assûré de leur Religion" (*Hist. cr. du V. T.*, Pref.). Credner, *Einleitung in d. N. T.*, I, p. 35. Beyond doubt, this motive played a relatively small part in Simon's life ; he was too great a scholar to give it large play. Still, the motive existed in him. In the average Roman Catholic apologete it was strong and lively, and the Protestants heard of it, in season and out of season. The history of the ancient doctrine of inspiration falls into three periods. (1) The formation of the conception in the Catholic Church. (2) The Middle Ages. The tendency toward an extreme doctrine was strong and steady (Hagenbach, *Dogmengeschichte, s. v.* "Inspiration"; Schaff, *Hist. of Christian Church*, IV, pp. 613, 614). (3) The sixteenth century. The Romanists made a specialty of the idea of the Church and so eased up on the theory of inspiration. The Protestants exalted the Scriptures above the Church and so made a specialty of the doctrine of inspiration.

[2] *Appar. Crit.* (2d ed., 1763), p. 634.

eighteenth century, he was, perforce, a man of reason.
He had no dogma of Church authority to lean upon
with one arm, while, with the other, he should deal
freely with the various readings. So his reverence
for God's Word compelled him to take reason into his
service and, no matter what the pain he met, to toil
through the mass of variants into clear opinions regarding the original text. The labours of a long line of
scholars have carried our methods and our materials
far beyond Bengel's standpoint. Our conception of
inspiration does not expose us to the mental distress
which he and the Protestants of his time had to
undergo. But the object of the Lower Criticism is
the same for us as for him. Piety and reason con-
spire to set up the ideal of the pure original text
as the inspiration and reward of scholarly devotion.[1]

The "Higher Criticism."   The old theory of inspiration having broken down,
and the "Lower Criticism" having taken the field,
the "Higher Criticism" could not long lag behind.
Similar causes and similar conditions gave it an ideal
of similar quality. The original text of Apostolic
thought and feeling must be discovered.[2]

[1] Hort, in Westcott and Hort's "*New Testament*" (N.Y.,
1882), II, pp. 1–3.
[2] The necessity of the transition from the "Lower" to the
"Higher" Criticism was laid down plainly by Wetstein : "Si
libros N. T. planius et plenius intelligere cupis, indue personam
illorum, quibus primum ad legendum ab Apostolis traditi fue-
runt ; transfer te cogitatione in illud tempus et in illam regionem
ubi primum lect sunt . . . ad hæc præcipue attende, ubi in
locum incideris, unde te per systema hodiernum vel Theologiæ
vel Logicæ, aut per opiniones hodie receptas expedire non
potes." *Nov. T.* (Amstel, 1752), II. p. 878. Cf. Semler's words
in Credner, *Einleitung*, I, p. 44. Semler might have taken *indue personam illorum* for his motto. On the connection between
the breakdown of the ancient doctrine of inspiration and criticism, see Michaelis, *Introduction* (tr. from 4th ed. by Marsh),
I, pp. 72–78. "An inward sensation of the effects of the Holy

From the sixth century down, the body of knowledge concerning the New Testament was both narrow in scope and fixed in its outlines.[1] Time, piety, and ignorance — a mighty triumvirate — gave it a most imposing air of finality. It was accepted by all men as authentic and sufficient. Even the Reformation scholars accepted it, for the most part, without demur.[2] It was part and parcel of a sacred Tradition. By reason of the ideas wherewith it was connected, it gave Christians of all name mental satisfaction, putting their questions to rest. The little handful of facts which Cassiodorus gave to his monks had the authority of the Church or the inspiration of Scripture behind it. But when both these dogmas in their ancient form played the eighteenth-century Protestant false, he immediately felt the need of a larger range of facts regarding the New Testament books and of a more interior study of the books themselves. This interior study grew out of the desire to know the New Testament from the inside, to discover and fix its original meanings, the true text of its thought and feeling. The desire for a larger body of facts was born of the knowledge that the text of any

Traditional knowledge of the New Testament ceases to satisfy.

Ghost and the consciousness of the utility of these writings . . . I have never experienced it in the whole course of my life." So the question about inspiration gives way to the question about genuineness. A dogmatic question gives way to an historical one.

[1] The "Introduction" of Cassiodorus. A small body of opinions became stereotyped. For nearly a thousand years nobody felt the need of examining them, still less of going behind them.

[2] Bleek, *Introduction to N. T.*, I, pp. 16, 21. Luther was free in some of his judgments on Biblical questions. But his judgments, while they have considerable dogmatic interest, were a very slight contribution to historical study. On Bodenstein, see Credner, *Kanon*, p. 201 ff.

form of human experience cannot be taken away from the context of its time and place and remain wholly intelligible. The backbone, then, of Higher Criticism, as its history interprets it, was the resolution to know the mental and emotional text and context of the New Testament books.

Protestant-ism and Criticism.

Necessarily, the Higher Criticism could not be loyally developed save in a Protestant country. The Roman Catholic Church has given the world some great Biblical scholars. But something more than the work of occasional scholars was required, if the principle of the Higher Criticism was to be permanently established. A persistent, critical mood, that is, an intellectual temper which steadily impels men to push in behind traditions and legends, in order to verify or reject them, was demanded. The Roman Catholic Church, by reason of her doctrine of authority, could not supply the demand. Until she fundamentally changes her methods, she will reserve a large number of positions as being not open to question. Now, it is of no avail to permit men to think freely upon the Bible, if they will but go far enough with the authority of the Church. Human reason is an organic thing. It moves altogether, if it moves at all. Freedom to deal with the Bible cannot keep house with absolute obedience to an ecclesiastical body as its head. At best, the marriage between them is left-handed, or a marriage of convenience. The critical work of the Roman Catholic Church cannot but be half-hearted and unthorough. The Higher Criticism, both as a principle and as an achievement, must seek its fortune in a Protestant land.

Germany.

It fell to the lot of Germany to give the critical principle a home and provide its support. Holland, a leader of scholarship throughout the seventeenth century, had lost ground by the time that the critical mood came over Western Europe. England had done and was still to do master-work in the field of Lower Criticism. But by reason of what was worst, as well as what was best, in the England of 1750–1850, the chance there for free Bible-study was not great. The strength of the Anglican Church in matters ecclesiastical — like the strength of most English things — rested upon a compromise. The Bible was indeed exalted as the supreme, even the exclusive authority in ultimate questions. But, on the other hand, the English Church kept hold on the principle of Tradition. And in the third decade of our century, at the very time when Biblical criticism in Germany was reaching its crisis, the Oxford Movement gave to that principle increased prestige. As to the Dissenters, while their dogmatic position touching Holy Scriptures was clear and uncompromising, they lacked, in the eighteenth century, both the culture and the standing in the universities that was necessary, if men were to feel the full force of the mental movements of the epoch.

English Deism had seen some things to which England. orthodoxy was blind and had spoken its mind freely upon Biblical questions.[1] However, Deistic doubt did not run its full career in England. It was met and overcome, not so much by a mental as an emotional process, namely, the revival of religion through the Wesleyan and Evangelical Movement. Finally, the university life of England was at a low ebb.[2]

[1] Thus Toland in *Nazarenus, or Jewish, Gentile, and Mahometan Christianity* (1718), discovered that difference of parties in the primitive church which afterward played so momentous a part in the criticism of the N. T.

Upon the English Deist's views of Scripture, Leckler's *Gesch. d. Engl. Deismus*, 1841.

[2] Adam Smith's well-known opinion of the English universities: "Their laws and life arranged, not for the profit of the

Even in this particular, England's merit mingled with her failings. She was just entering upon that vast industrial expansion which ended by making her the mistress of the seas. This, together with her splendid political opportunities, drew so deeply upon her finest resources of purpose and character, that the academic life could not reach a relatively high position.

Conditions in Germany.

In Germany all these conditions were reversed. There the doubt of Deism, coming from England by way of France, ran its full career. No revival of religion cut it short. Pietism indeed played a considerable part, but it could not administer an emotional quietus to rational difficulties. It could temper criticism by causing sap to run into it from the religious tap-root of our being, but it could not choke off criticism nor postpone it. In Germany the eager, resolute, self-confident doubt which was so considerable a part of the eighteenth century's intellectual staple, was not fended off from the Bible. The traditional opinion about the Sacred Books and their authors caught its full force.

German philosophy.

Into the deepest mystery of a nation's being and work we may not hope to penetrate. To the marvellous mental movement of Germany during the period that began about 1750 we can assign many occasioning causes. Deeper than that we cannot go. Yet it is enough for our purpose to be assured of the fact. And the fact is certain. In the history of the mental experience of Europe, German philosophy is the only possible parallel to the philosophy of the Greeks. The splendid bloom of rational effort and philosophical

students, but for the ease and comfort of the teachers." Allowing for his exaggeration, it is clear that the mental life of the English universities from 1750 to 1830 compares very poorly with the German universities.

achievement between 1780 and 1840 was indeed short-lived, when compared with the long career of philosophy in Greece. But in power, and reach, and scope it is every way worthy to be compared with the best Greece can show.

Inasmuch as philosophy is the layman's interpretation of man's life and world, it should be clear that the place where modern philosophy did the great bulk of its work was likely to be the place where the final questions regarding the Bible, its nature and its root in history, could be driven home. Germany, the land of philosophy, was the land of a masterful mental force that would not let any object, however great or imposing, plead the benefit of clergy.[1] As the Canon Law had yielded to the power of the State, so that men in orders were judged by the same courts that tried lay cases, so now, the old barriers between rational investigation and the Scriptures having broken wholly down, the entire body of Scriptural fact and interpretation came under examination.

The German university indicated the completion of the mental revolution which had begun at the Renaissance. The control of education now passes out of the hands of the clergy. The secular power, the State, assumes it. This means that the discussion of sacred things shall be carried on as secular studies

The German university.

---

[1] The "secularisation" of education is a matter very close to the history of N. T. criticism. For the bias and control of education shows plainly what is the centre of interest and what are the methods of studying the things that are interesting. The aim of modern teaching is to overcome the *divortium rerum et verborum*, to get the mind close to reality, to the original texts of nature and history.

Paulsen, *Gesch. d. gelehrt. Unter.*; Arnoldt, *F. A. Wolff*, II, pp. 1–30; "International Education Series," ed. by W. T. Harris; Raumer, *Gesch. d. Pädagogik*, 3d Th., 2d Abtheil, p. 152; Herman Schiller, *Gesch. d. Pädagogik*, 1891.

H

are carried on — by free research.   The modern university is the embodiment of the modern or critical principles of insistence upon the original facts of nature and history, and upon nothing but the facts. The university was a mental workshop of a new kind. Here the new learning had its stronghold.   The outlying objects of knowledge could here keep up a constant attack upon reason, preventing the formation of fixed and unchanging hypotheses.   Here the universe presses steadily upon the mind, forcing it to keep open house to new ideas and impressions.   The very atmosphere of the modern university is critical. Nothing can stay its mental impetus toward original research.[1]

Theology in the university.

Hither came theology to make or lose its fortune. This was in keeping with the Reformation principle. The theological seminary, as a place isolated and detached, must be abandoned.   Theology, the study of the most sacred things, must think out its system in close communion with the vigorous and tumultuous mental life of the modern world.[2]   And hither came our Sacred Books, freely exposing themselves to the questions and the cross-questions of the free reason. They had entered into a temporary alliance with the mediæval hierarchy.   They now chose for themselves interpreters of a different school.   "The Reformation," says Holtzmann, "signifies a critical act which

---

[1] Paulsen, *The German University.*

[2] Paulsen, *op. cit.*, pp. 226, 227 ; Kuyper, *Encyclopædia of Sacred Theology* (tr. 1898), p. 626.   Compare upon the history of seminary education in the Roman Catholic Church, Von Schulte, *Can. Recht*, Bd. III, 1er Th., p. 281, and Paulsen, *German Universities*, p. 105.   In the Protestant churches of America, the theological seminaries have been more or less isolated.   But this is, on the whole, not so much the expression of a deliberate policy as the result of position and circumstance.

the spirit of Christianity, coming to itself and going deep into its own nature, exercises upon its entire past."[1] In the German university the Reformation principle could be followed home.

[1] *Einleitung i. d. N. T.*, 1886, p. 175.

CHAPTER VI

PRELIMINARY WORK OF THE HIGHER CRITICISM[1]

Richard
Simon.

RICHARD SIMON, the Roman Catholic scholar († 1712), has been honoured by Protestant scholars with the title "Father of Modern Biblical Study." [2] They do honour to their own impartiality by thus honouring him. But the correctness of the title may be doubted. That he was a very great scholar is beyond dispute. That he contributed largely to the material and spirit of criticism is equally beyond dispute.[3] And it may seem a waste of time to debate over the correctness of an epithet. Still, an epithet conveys an opinion. If it is to be given at all, it should be given to the right

[1] Literature: Semler's *Leben* (autobiography); Vincent, *Hist. of Textual Criticism*, 1899; the sections on the history of Introduction in Reuss, *Hist. of the N. T.*, tr. 1884; Holtzmann, *Einleitung in d. N. T.*, 1886; Mangold's ed. of Bleek's *Einleitung;* Bacon, *Introd. to the N. T.* One of the best short histories is found in Credner, *Einleitung*, 1836.

[2] Bleek, I, p. 17; Credner, *Einleitung*, I, § 24.

[3] Simon expresses the spirit and aim of modern criticism with perfect clearness: " Si je n'ay pas suivy la methode des Theologiens Scholastiques, c'est que je l'ay trouvée peu sure. J'ay taché autant qu'il m'a été possible de ne rien avancer qui ne fût appuyé sur de bons Actes : au lieu que la Theologie de l'école nous fait quelquefois douter des choses les plus certaines. La Religion consistant principalement en des choses de fait, les subtilites de ces Theologiens qui n'ont pas en une connaissance exacte de l'antiquité," etc. (*Hist. cr. du Texte du N. T.*, Preface).

man. And Simon, great as he was, cannot be called, with literal accuracy, the Father of criticism. For the gist of criticism consists in the direct application of scientific methods to the study of our Sacred Books, without regard to authority of any kind, with no concern save to know the Bible as it is in itself and in its history. Criticism is not primarily a body of material nor an apparatus, but a temperament; and the essence of the temperament is the free study of the Scriptural Canon. To this point Simon did not come. His opinions, however they might seem to break with the traditional conception of the Canon, remained, at least as far as form went, within its precincts.

The title, if given at all, should rather be bestowed on Semler. For in him the critical principle found a direct application to the ultimate question of Biblical study. Since the fourth century the Canon had stood before the mind and imagination as a finished total, a mystical unity free from the suggestion of internal differences and external changes. Memory of the debates, through which opinion regarding certain books had passed, utterly perished. The primary work of the Church, even in the Nicene age, was not Biblical scholarship. It was anything but a critical age. Its function was dogmatic theology rather than interpretation. Fixed positions, finished statements, were its end. Far more was this the case after the fourth century. So, when once the limits of the Canon had been settled, the dominant mood of the Church suppressed the ideas of process and change. In the course of a few centuries the impression of the Canon's divine immutability had so far deepened that the Bible confronted the mind as a thing so majestic that no man durst question it. Semler.

The Lower Criticism nibbled at the edges of the ultimate question regarding the Canon. Work like

Simon's penetrated far into it.   But it remained for Semler to go to the centre.

A typical scholar's life.

Semler's life typifies the entire critical process of the eighteenth century.[1]   He was born in 1725.   His father being a scholar of rank, he grew up within scholarly surroundings.   To judge by what he himself tells us in his autobiography, his life falls into three periods.   At the outset of his mental career he had a very strong bent toward the study of the "Humanities," history and the classics.   Then he came under the influence of pietism, and his interest in the Humanities was checked.[2]   The study of theology and Scripture seemed the only thing.   Finally, before he got through the university, the Humanities returned in triumph.   When, in 1754, he became professor, and began to lecture upon Biblical subjects, he marked out the path of historical study.   He had already gone through and come out of the alarms raised by the various readings.   He now entered — and he was the pioneer — the field of Higher Criticism.

In his first course of lectures he took the principles of exegesis as his theme.   He found fault with exist-

---

[1] The student should make a detailed study of Semler's life and work.   In his autobiography (*Leben*, 1781), he gives us a clear eighteenth-century account of himself.   The three periods: (1) He had a strong inclination to the "Humanities," *i.e.* to broad historical study of the classics.   (2) Pietism got control of him and his interest in the "Humanities" declined (*Leben*, I, p. 96).   (3) His old love returned, the "Humanities" triumphed (II, pp. 11–120).   Having already passed through the terrors of the "Lower Criticism" (II, pp. 124–126), he was ripe for the "Higher."   For the essence of the Higher Criticism is the application to the Sacred Books of those principles of historical study into which the "Humanities" had led Semler.   For Semlér's general historical studies, see Hase, *Kirchengesch.*, 1885, 1er Th., p. 41.

[2] The pietistic attitude toward "secular" learning, Hagenbach, § 277 ; Schiller, *Gesch. d. Pädagogik*, pp. 201, 202.

ing methods; they stuck too close to the devotional and dogmatic lines of interpretation. True interpretation must be historical. The student must cut loose from temporary needs and go back into the period when the Sacred Books originated, and seek a clear knowledge of the ideas of the time, both the author's ideas and those of his contemporaries as well. In this way he shall see things as they are.

Semler expressly says that he took his exegetical principles from the Humanities.[1] He thus exemplifies the final stage in the process of criticism. We have seen (Ch. III) how the Scriptures came to be practically and theoretically isolated. We remember (Ch. IV) how the first steps were taken to overcome this isolation. The infallibility of the Church was rejected, a first-hand knowledge of Holy Writ was demanded, and the new learning — the learning of self-respecting reason — rose to honour. In Semler the new learning came into direct contact with the Scriptures, and the critical principle in Bible-study was the result.

"The Humanities."

In 1771 he published his *Treatise on the Free Investigation of the Canon*.[2] The very title advertised the new principle. Semler proved that the traditional conception of the building of the Canon was mistaken. The Canon was not made at a stroke. On the contrary, it took centuries to fix its limits. The opinions of the ancient Church were not uniform. On the contrary, the churches of Alexandria, Antioch, and Jerusalem differed regarding certain books. Even in the same church, opinions touching individual authors changed; the church of Rome, for example, did not

"Free investigation of the Canon."

[1] "*Aus humanioribus*" are his own words (*Leben*, I, pp. 208, 209).

[2] *Abhandlung von freier Untersuchung des Canon*, 1771; *Apparatus ad lib. interp. N. T.*, 1767.

always think alike about the Apocalypse. Thus the idea of immutability was dislodged from the conception of the Canon.

It now became evident that the process out of which the doctrine of the Canon issued was an historical and human process. Like everything historical, it must be studied. And the study must be free, with an eye single in its devotion to the facts as they happened. Patient and fearless investigation is the privilege and duty of Christian scholarship.

Differences found within the New Testament. Semler also called attention to differences within the New Testament literature. He perceived the unlikeness between Jewish and Pauline Christianity. For sixteen hundred years the New Testament had been thought of as a divine book. The authoritative theory of inspiration made it impossible for the human to retain its individuality in the immediate presence of the divine. So the acceptation of the New Testament as the canonic expression of God's mind could not go along with the belief that the New Testament authors reasoned as men must always reason, unless they would unman themselves. The Sacred Books could not admit differences. Everywhere they must have the same colour of feeling and thought. But when the ancient theory of inspiration had fallen, the facts in the case presented themselves to the eye. Semler saw what Baur at a later day made so much of. In other ways, also, he suggested the lines of subsequent study. And, in a word, he insisted that the Sacred Books must be studied as human books.

That statement in itself is a very simple one. It gives us, however, the end and aim of improved Bible-study. Semler, in effect, published the news of a mental revolution.[1] To study the Sacred Books as

[1] Credner, *Einleitung*, I, p. 43.

human books was to study them historically.   And to
study them historically was to make them their own
interpreters.

The Reformation principle required that the simple, historical sense of Scripture should be sovereign.
Only so could the supremacy of Scripture be successfully asserted.   For, unless the simple sense is taken
as the final sense, the allegorical method, driven out
at the front door, enters at the back door.   And, until
allegory is wholly gotten rid of, the Scriptures cannot
be self-interpreting.

The life of Semler serves to remind us that the
Higher Criticism is not primarily an analysis of docu-
ments nor a study of literary problems, but the final
chapter in the history of interpretation.   Semler,
passing from the Lower Criticism to the Higher, began
his work by lecturing on exegesis.   At the outset, he
saw the necessity of taking the New Testament into
the climate and circumstances of the Apostolic age.
Interpretation must be grammatical.   And grammar
must cease to be at the mercy of dogma.   The intrinsic meanings of the New Testament language must be
the final aim of study.[1]   But grammar alone does not
suffice.[2]   Interpretation must be historical.   The stu-

---

[1] For the history of N. T. Grammar, Winer, *N. T. Gr.* (tr. by
Thayer), *Introduction*, 8ᵉ Auf. by Schmiedel, 1894, §§ 1, 2 ;
Reuss, *Hist. of N. T.*, II, p. 591 ; Cave, *Introduction to Theology*, pp. 323, 324 ; Diestel, *Gesch. d. A. T.*, pp. 150, 620–626,
636 ; Paulsen, *Gesch. d. gelehrten Unter.*, pp. 543–545 ; *Realencyclopädie*, VI, p. 290 *sq.*

Naturally, the principles of grammar come into N. T. study
from the outside.   Theology tyrannised over the thought of
Scripture to such an extent that they could not grow up from
within.

[2] The connection between " Criticism " and interpretation is
illustrated by the history of the phrase " Grammatical-Historical Interpretation " which established itself between 1750 and

dent must realise the mental conditions both of the New Testament writers and of the men to whom they wrote. Going further, Semler brought to light the fact that the Church's doctrine of the Canon was a growth; and he suggested that the New Testament literature itself, as a human literature, was likewise a growth. Thus he pointed out the way into the Higher Criticism as the free study of the origins and the literary relationship of our New Testament books. All the while, however, the object was true interpretation. And we must not permit the manifold departments of Biblical study in our own time to blind us to the fact that this is the final aim of criticism in all its forms.

Michaelis.

The first systematic "Introduction" of a modern kind was published by Michaelis, in 1750. The contrast between this and the Introduction of Cassiodorus, in the sixth century, — the standard book for nearly a thousand years, — is very instructive. The body of data is vastly larger. This fact, by itself, betokens the coming change. For the motive of knowledge and its material always interact. A growing body of data indicates an increasing pressure upon the mental framework approved by Tradition. Again, in the eighteenth-century book scientific curiosity plays a very considerable part, while in the sixth-century book it did not exist. Michaelis has an eager desire

1800 as the only correct description of interpretative methods. The *Selbstbiographie* of Bretschneider gives us light. See also Bretschneider's *Auslegung d. N. T.* (1806). He calls Ernesti the father of the true grammatical interpretation, but finds fault with him on the ground that he lacked the broad knowledge of the thought and feeling of N. T. times (he calls it " dogmengeschichte ") which is essential to a " N. T. Times " (p. 10). On the use of "Introduction," see Bacon, *Introduction to the N. T.*, chs. 1, 2.

to know all that it is possible to know regarding the New Testament literature; and the possession of a scholarly method insures a steady growth of knowledge. And, finally, whereas with Cassiodorus the ancient doctrine of inspiration is in the vigour of youth, with Michaelis it is drawing its last breath. He put forth four editions of his book (1750–1788). The body of facts grows larger. The emphasis upon inspiration weakens. The interior criticism — the so-called "Higher Criticism" — feels firmer ground beneath its foot.

Problems now appeared. So long as Tradition reigned, there could be no real problems connected with the New Testament, because the real facts in the case could not force themselves into notice. But between 1750 and 1800 the facts began to come under the eye. Problems arose forthwith. *Problems appear.*

The Synoptical Problem, or the question touching the relations between the first three Gospels, attracted attention. To Irenæus, in the second century, each Gospel was an eternal type of evangelical truth. Literary relationship between them, if it existed, was almost as insignificant, as incapable of drawing and holding curiosity, as speculation upon the literary connection between Plato's *Ideas*. When, however, the New Testament books came within reach of scientific methods, it became necessary to ask for an explanation of their striking likeness and their almost equally striking diversity.[1] *Synoptical question.*

---

[1] Tatian's *Diatessaron* did not aim at a " harmony "; it was a history, of the ancient Oriental sort, and was intended to put more or less out of use the authorities upon which it was based (Professor G. Moore, *Journal of Bib. Lit.*, 1890 ; Wildeboer, *Die Lit. d. A. T.* (1895), pp. 3, 4). Irenæus contended for the immovableness of the truth proclaimed by the Church (1. 9. 5, 10 ; 3. 3). The thought of difference within the Gospels was beyond

The Book of Acts suggested questions. In 1798 Paulus, following a hint of Semler, took the position that it was written with a dogmatic purpose, to defend the Apostle Paul against the attacks of the strict Jewish-Christian party. A generation later, this idea, taken up by Baur, became fruitful both of truth and of error. The interest attaching to it here is found in the treatment of the book as related to the movements of mind and antagonisms of belief in the Apostolic age. It thus suggested the necessity of studying the New Testament as a literature in vital relation with historical forces.

The Pauline Epistles began to be treated as real letters, addressed to concrete situations and specific circumstances. They bear that character on their face. But the Church had been unable to see it. They had been regarded as timeless books, possessing the right of free entry into all situations. Rightly taken, that is deeply true. All great books are timeless. The New Testament books are supremely so. None the less, they are related to concrete situations. They are timeless because they went so deep into time.

his reach ; they are four in number and could not have been more or less (3. 11) ; each is perfect after its kind. This state of opinion continued until the sixteenth century. Osiander first used the title " Harmony " in 1537. The thought of difference between the Gospels and of difficulty in harmonising the differences now appeared. But in the first period of the modern Harmony, the defence was vastly stronger than the attack ; the ancient idea of inspiration prevented the discovery of any literary problem. The *Wolfenbüttel Fragments* (issued by Lessing, 1773–1781) proclaimed the end of the long reign of that idea. The title of Evanson's book, *The Dissonance of the Four Gospels*, etc., 1792, is significant. Michaelis published in 1783 his *Erklärung der Begrabniss u. Auferstehungs Geschichte Christi nach d. vier Evangelisten.* The modern period of Gospel Criticism had begun. The relation of the Synoptists had become a literary problem.

They are free of space because they took some one part of space with divine seriousness. St. Paul's epistles are as truly letters as those of Cicero and Pliny. And the dawning conception of them as letters showed that the historical study of the New Testament was well started.

Still, the criticism of this period, taken as a whole, was uncertain in aim. It had the vagueness of work done during a mental interregnum, when one great conception has been dethroned and its successor has not yet been crowned. The New Testament books were no longer treated as if they possessed an exclusively divine character. The human authors of Scripture were now in plain view. Yet the new principle of study was not followed to its larger issues.

The criticism of this period unsure in its aim.

Meanwhile, Germany had entered an epoch grandly creative both in literature and philosophy. Lessing, Schiller, and Goethe on the one hand, Kant, Fichte, and Hegel on the other, gave strength and spirit to the imagination, depth and scope to reason. Noble feeling and resolute thought were interpreting human life at large. How should they interpret the Scriptures?

The study of the Old Testament was the first to be affected. In England, Marsh, treating the Hebrew poetry in a poetical way, had already indicated the coming change. In Germany, Herder, superior to Marsh both in genius and mental freedom, made the Old Testament seem contemporary to the doubters of his time. He humanised it. The study of the New Testament had to wait a while longer. But the delay was sure to be short. All signs pointed to the quarter whence the fresh wind was to blow.[1]

Herder.

[1] The eighteenth century is the explanation of nineteenth-century criticism. Biblical criticism is part of a great common movement of European life and mind. And in that movement

the eighteenth century is the point of precipitation. The first main feature of the century is that the intellectual enthusiasm of the Occident now begins to run in a channel entirely independent of that in which religious enthusiasm runs. The active reason becomes wholly free in its attitude toward theology and Tradition. The second main feature is that a considerable part of religious enthusiasm now begins to run in a social channel. These two things, working together, brought about in the nineteenth century a thorough change of climate for the interpretation of that total human past of which the Bible forms the canonic part.

CHAPTER VII

THE TURNING-POINT IN THE HISTORY OF CRITICISM [1]

THE complete breach with Tradition, brought about
by the eighteenth century, enabled the facts of sacred
history to triumph over dogma. For the time being,
the New Testament suffered. Its mysteries were
paraphrased in terms of common sense. Its visions
were brought down to the level of earnest, but prosaic,
morality. The miraculous, translated into the language of the day, turned out to be an emotional interpretation of commonplace events.[2] Still, the price
paid for freedom was not too high. Now, at last, it
was possible for the Scriptures to be known as they
are in themselves. Reason, unfettered, even auda-
cious, might lay unconsecrated hands on the Ark of
God. Yet, when all is said, the eighteenth-century
rationalist was not more extreme on one side of interpretation than the ideal Pope of the Middle Ages was
on the other. Neither gave the sacred text its

Facts get
the better
of dogma.

[1] Literature : Zeller, *David Friedrich Strauss*, tr. 1874, and
"Ferdinand Christian Baur," in *Vorträge u. Abhandlungen*,
1875, Vol. I ; Schwartz, *Geschichte d. neuesten Theologie*, 3e
Auf., 1864 ; Pfleiderer, *The Philosophy of Religion*, tr. 1887,
Vol. II ; Baur, *Geschichte d. Christ. Kirche*, 5r band (1862);
Flint, *Philosophy of History* (France), 1894 ; Laurent, *Hist. d.
l'Humanité*, Vol. XVI.

[2] De Wette, *Theodore oder des Zweifler's Weihe* (1822), I,
pp. 20, 21. This "novel" is well worth reading as a part of
the mental history of a great scholar who passed through the
critical years in the history of criticism.

rights.   But the rationalist provided the negative condition for the true understanding of the Bible.   A fearless reason, insisting that the need of knowledge is as fundamental as the need of salvation, and that all facts are sacred and have a divine right to be studied from within, had acquired in the field of Bible-study a position of vantage from which it could not be dislodged.

Criticism in need of a controlling principle.

Down to 1835, however, the Higher Criticism lacked a controlling principle.   Much good work was done. Many suggestive beginnings were made.   But, on the whole, it was a period of piecemeal study.   An organising conception, one that should give unity of view and coördination of results, had not yet appeared.

The defects of the period may be best seen in De Wette, because in him the critical virtues of the time were at their highest point.[1] He had a clear and fearless mind, a wide knowledge of facts, a masterly power of presentation, fine literary taste, a piercing judgment joined with deep religious feeling.   Yet his studies of the New Testament were mainly individual studies held together by the traditional conception of the Canon.   The old dogmatic view of the Canon had gone.   The habit of treating the New Testament books as a body of literature set off by itself remained. This was an inconsistency.   The Church had drawn up an authoritative list of books.   The books it can-onised were believed to be of apostolic origin.   Their inspiration gave them all a common character.   They constituted an organism, a spiritual body.   Each book

New Testament studies loosely related.

---

[1] De Wette († 1849) was a man of letters and a theologian as well as a Biblical scholar, an all-round mind, free from much of the inherent narrowness of the specialists of a later genera-tion.   He possessed in high degree the clear-headed mental sobri-ety which was characteristic of Bretschneider and other scholars whose habits were fixed before 1835.

was bound to all the others by the tie of a common divine nature.

The Church did not need to know the literary connection between one book and another. Neither did she need to know the concrete historical situation to which this or that book attached itself, nor the broad, historical background of the New Testament as a whole. The sole, decisive question touching any portion of the Canon was, Did an Apostle or an Apostolic man write it?[1] An affirmative answer assured its footing within the Canon. And once there, no questions concerning its literary pedigree or its historical belongings needed to be asked. Indeed, they could not be asked. For the dogma of inspiration not only gave mystical unity to the New Testament, conceived as an organism of saving truth, but it so isolated it, so separated it from human literature, that such questions became a mental impossibility.

Bible-study had a real unity, a controlling principle. The Sacred Books were nearer to each other than a man's mind and body, more clearly coherent than the parts of a noble statue. The mind of their common, their Divine Author held them together. Down to the Reformation, therefore, Bible-study could not be fragmentary. And even in the Reformation period it suffered no loss of unity. Ecclesiastical infallibility had been discarded. Biblical infallibility, however, remained. The human author of Scripture had not yet come into view. The magnificent enthusiasm for the pure Word of God, the exalted sense of its inspiration, kept every part of the New Testament in vital touch with every other part. All

Dogma of inspiration gave unity to older Bible-study.

---

[1] The principle of Apostolic authorship was not always carried out, but it was the intention. Cf. Holtzmann, *Einleitung*, pp. 134–160. Weiss, *Einleitung* (2e Auf.), pp. 34, 64.

I

the results of interpretation were related. Nothing was detached.

But when the ancient doctrine of inspiration decayed, Bible-study became piecemeal. Thus De Wette, having given up the Pauline authorship of the Pastoral Epistles, left them adrift, as if they were literary fragments. The reason was twofold. Or, rather, it was one reason under two aspects. In the first place, throughout a period of sixteen hundred years, the sole question regarding any given New Testament book had been one of apostolic origin. It was perfectly natural, then, that for a considerable time after the downfall of Tradition — 1750 to 1835 — that question should continue to be decisive. Hence, when De Wette — herein thoroughly representative [1] — settled the question of Pauline authorship against the Pastorals, he seemed to have done all that the case required. In the second place, the New Testament books having been so long bound together and thought together by an overmastering dogma, the critical studies of the New Testament books appeared to have a unity which in reality they lacked. The shell of the old dogma held them together and gave them vital relation and coherence. But in truth, from the critical point of view, this was no better than a mechanical unity. For criticism calls for an historical treatment of the New Testament literature.

Mechanical unity.

---

[1] It is the point of view of Michaelis, Eichhorn, Hug, Credner, etc. Haenlein's *Introduction* (1794) will give the student a fair conception of the purpose and scope of that period in scholarship. The question of genuineness had supplanted the dogma of inspiration. This holds good on the radical as well as on the conservative side of scholarship, *e.g.* Evanson's *Dissonance of the Four Gospels and the Evidence of their Respective Authenticity examined* (1792). But that question was only the halfway house to a truly historical study.

Suppose the debate over Apostolic authorship to have gone against a given book. That is not enough. We desire to know its relation to the great movement that lies back of the New Testament as a whole. A human, literary unity must take the place of the bare dogmatic unity.

We do not mean to say that, down to 1835, there was no attempt to give the New Testament books a local habitation and a human name, after the questions of apostolic authorship had been settled one way or the other. There are hints and suggestions in De Wette. In Gieseler's treatise on the Gospels, the synoptical question opens the door into the study of conditions and movements within the Apostolic Church.[1] Bretschneider, in his treatise on the Fourth Gospel, after he had rejected the Johannine authorship, proceeded to discuss the characteristics of Judaism with which, as he thought, the book concerned itself; and ended by giving the Fourth Gospel an historical habitat early in the second century.[2] Credner urged the need of apprehending the general mental condition of the Apostolic age.[3] Yet the only application of it he made was to condemn the notion that the Christians of the first century ascribed to the authors of our New Testament books any extraordinary inspiration.

On the whole, Schleiermacher's essay on 1 Timothy (1807) is representative of the methods of this period.

Suggestions of a more historical method.

Schleiermacher on 1 Timothy.

[1] Gieseler, *Versuch über die Entwickelung u. die frühesten Schicksale der Schriftlichen Evangelien* (1818).

[2] Bretschneider, *Probabilia de Evangelii et Epistolarum Joannis Apostoli indole et origine*, 1820. A model of sobriety and restraint. The specific reference is to chapter 4. Upon Bretschneider, Watkins, *The Fourth Gospel* (1890), pp. 179–190.

[3] Credner, *Beiträge z. Einleitung in d. bib. Schriften* (1832), I, p. 7, " *die gesammtanschauung der Apostolischen Zeit.*"

He went through the letter in detail. He compared its style and use of words with Paul's usage in the other epistles. He criticised the vocabulary, the turn of thought, and finally decided against the genuineness of the letter.[1] There he stopped. Beyond this question of genuineness the scholars of the time did not go. It is well within bounds to say that, down to 1835, the critical study of the New Testament was fragmentary. De Wette is typical. He gives us an aggregate of fine observations and suggestive conclusions. But that is all. There is no unifying principle, no controlling or coördinating view. We have a number of detached essays, joined together by the fact that they deal with different portions of a literature which the Church of the third and fourth centuries was pleased to canonise.

Forces at work upon a new conception.

Yet, throughout the first years of the eighteenth century, and even earlier, forces were at work which paved the way for a conception that should give coherence and order to the results of critical study. It was that idea of humanity which is the ruling idea of our time.[2] So long as theology was the queen of

---

[1] Schleiermacher, *Ueber den sogenannten ersten Brief des Paulus an den Timotheos*, 1807.

[2] Edgar Quinet, *Le Christianisme et la revolution française*, 1845 ; Laurent, *Hist. de l'Humanité*, XVI ; Hettner, *Literaturgesch. d. achtzehnten Jahr.*, III, 3, abth. 2 ; Stopford Brooke, *Theology in the English Poets;* Morley, *Rousseau;* Baur, *Christ. Kirche*, V, pp. 41–45 ; R. Haym, *Herder*, 1880–1885 ; Otto Pfleiderer, *Philosophy of Religion*, I, pp. 203–225 ; Bluntschli, *Staatswörterbuch*, VI, p. 428.

The story of the building of the idea of Humanity is as important for our knowledge of our own time as is the building of the idea of the primitive family and tribe for our understanding of the men of antiquity. Cf. Coulanges, *La Cité Antique* (ed. of 1895); Hearn, *The Aryan Household*, 1891 ; Maine, *Ancient Law;* Robertson Smith, *The Religion of the Semites*, 2d ed., Lect. 2.

reason, the idea of God overbore the idea of humanity. It will help us at this point to remember once more that the history of Bible-study is just one aspect of a much vaster history. We cannot separate it from the general movement of Christian experience. So we need to keep clearly in mind the fact that the main characteristic of Bible-study down to the eighteenth century was in unison with the temper and disposition of Christian thought as a whole. Theology was the main concern of deep-minded men. Now, the theology of that time, with all its great merits, had one very serious fault. It made the idea of God altogether too transcendent. Just as, in practice, the picked men and women thought it necessary to go outside the bounds of the common life, and to coöperate with one another through a monastic organisation, in order to become intimate with God; so, in theory, the best thought of the time deemed it necessary to exalt the idea of God above history in order to insure its purity and majesty. As long as the tendency lasted, the idea of God overpowered the idea of humanity.

The idea of humanity in old theology.

Nevertheless, the genius of Christianity demanded that the idea of humanity should be as deeply emphasised as the idea of God. Upon any other footing, the Biblical view of revelation is undone. And within the institutions of the Church, even when they were most monastic, were tendencies that exalted our nature. Even her errors leaned in this direction. The worship of the Virgin, the coronation of the Papacy, were indirect ways of magnifying the capacity of the race. And the ideal of a Catholic communion, mistaken as its expressions sometimes were, and perverted its methods, drew its sap from the inmost being of Christianity. For our religion is bottomed upon the most impassioned faith in the spiritual unity of

Christianity and humanity.

mankind; since, without this, the unity of God were an empty theological formula. To an equal degree is it built upon an impassioned faith in the spiritual capacity of our nature. The doctrines of the Incarnation and the Kingdom of God refuse to have it otherwise.

When, therefore, the idea of humanity came on the field of Biblical study, it was not at all the case that the Sacred Books of Christianity were given over to the tender mercies of an alien. On the contrary, we find herein a striking illustration of the truth that God comes to his goal by roads which his children, in the omniscience of their ignorance, consider aimless and roundabout. The idea of humanity is, in the main, a creation of the Christian religion. But it had to break away from the control of dogmatic Christianity in order to gain self-confidence. It found a mighty ally in the Humanities, the study of the knowledge and inspiration given by God along lines outside the education and experience of Israel. With the State, rising into dignity and power, it struck a covenant. Then, grown strong, and even overbearing, it went back to study the Scriptures. So far as appearances are concerned, it came from outside. In reality, it came from within. When tempered and chastened, it was to manifest itself as the spirit of Christ in modern men communing with the spirit of Christ in the Scriptures.

Idea of humanity in eighteenth century.

Great conceptions form slowly. But, after the long preparatory stages have elapsed, the final touches are quickly given. For seventeen hundred years the Biblical view of history and life, aided by the ideal elements in Greek and Roman culture, pressed steadily upon the mind of the Occident. An idea new to the world's thought was formed. In the eighteenth century it was clearly expressed. Rousseau preached it with contagious passion.[1] Herder carried it into the study of history. The Revolution made it a social programme. Through the poets it passed into the blood of Europe.

When we look back from the Revolution to the Renaissance, we become aware of a mighty change. In the earlier period the term "Humanity" denoted a new kind of literary interest, the eager study of the Classics, the appropriation of the food for thought and admiration furnished by the Greeks and Romans, in distinction from the food so long provided by theology. But in the days of Rousseau and Herder and Kant, the term stood for a creed. The sense of humanity had become, in effect, a religion.

The Renaissance and the Revolution.

If we have not already seen that the history of the Higher Criticism is the story of something far larger than a scholastic process, we should see it now. The specific results of criticism have been made possible by the existence of a body of academic students, broadly separated — as in Germany — from pressing practical problems, possessing leisure, and sitting at ease, for the most part, regarding the absorbing tasks and grinding institutional necessities of a great Church.[2] But the deeper causes of criticism have been collective forces, forces that are part and parcel of the total life of the Occident. Neither the divine

[1] See Kant, ed. Erdmann (4th), pp. 18, 19. Kant was deeply influenced by Rousseau. He strikes a new note for the motive of philosophy as well as for its method. The critical philosophy is to be the servant of Humanity.

[2] Stretching our words a little, we might venture to say that there are two main types of churchmen. There is the man whose chief concern is the creation and maintenance of institutions. And there is the man whose primary interest is speculation, the free play of thought. Palestinian and Alexandrian Judaism give us illustrations from ancient times. In modern times, examples abound.

necessity of criticism nor its actual course can be appreciated, if we insist upon treating it as wholly an affair of the school.

This fact stands out plainly from the genealogy of the great conception that was to give unity and coherence to the work of the New Testament scholars. It was given to them out of hand by the deepest spiritual tendencies of the eighteenth century. The genius of Christianity conceived the idea of humanity. The breakdown of Church authority, the breach with Tradition, the decay of theology, brought it to the birth. And the rise of the State to spiritual dignity, the ennobling of the secular interests of mankind, the discovery and majesty of the visible universe, by giving new meaning and scope to the terrestrial experience of man, provided the field and climate for its growth and prestige.

Hegelian philosophy.

The philosophy of Hegel endowed the new idea with an efficient organ. For in him German philosophy, self-confident and masterful, refusing to recognise as divine anything that did not make itself organic to the human, turned back to interpret the entire experience of the race. He viewed human experience in its totality. He conceived history as its autobiography. Every book handed down by the past, whether labelled "secular" or "sacred," must be treated as the record of a genuinely human experience. And nothing is fragmentary. The literature of a nation, the literature of a period, constitutes an organism. The individual's thoughts, to be intelligible, must be interpreted as part of a body of thought. Thus Hegel planned a new department of study, — the Philosophy of History.[1]

[1] On the history of the philosophy of history, Flint, book quoted; also his *Vico ;* and Laurent, *Hist. de l'Humanité*, XVIII. It is an interesting fact that the first edition of Vico's *Scienza*

For our purpose, it does not matter how largely certain parts of it resemble a fairy story, nor how high the hand wherewith Hegel shapes facts to the liking of his theory. We are concerned solely with the fact that the Philosophy of History was the theoretic expression of the idea of humanity and with the attendant fact that Hegel included within his plan the entire movement recorded and attested by the Scriptures.

Here was the organising principle, the controlling and coördinating conception for which criticism had been waiting. After 1750 the emphasis upon the human authors of the New Testament books steadily gained strength. When Eichhorn, in 1804, laid down the rule, "The New Testament writings are to be read as human books and tested in human ways," [1] scholarly opinion had ripened far enough to give it a frank adherence. But, as the case of Eichhorn himself — to say nothing of Schleiermacher, Bretschneider, and De Wette — clearly proves, the rule did not give coherence to Bible-study. In its application, it was a rule of literary method rather than a principle of broad, historical interpretation.

The organising principle of criticism.

Hegel's contribution to Bible-study — not the less significant because it was indirect — lay in the fact that he carried the philosophical idea of humanity into the field of Biblical interpretation. Revelation is to be thought of as a genuinely human process. The Words of God are spoken and His thoughts worked out within the precincts of human consciousness. The

Hegel's contribution to Bible-study.

Nuova issued in 1725, the second in 1732. The philosophical interpretation of history began at the same time with the outburst of the criticism of historical sources. On the naïve faith of Hegelianism in its own infallibility, cf. Trendelenburg, *Beiträge z. Phil.*, 1846, p. ix.

[1] In Holtzmann, *Einleitung*, p. 184.

New Testament, then, must be treated as a thoroughly human book.   Furthermore, it must be treated as the product of a human life.   And since the life realised itself as a total, all its parts being interknit, the literature of the life must be regarded as an organism.

Organic view of things.

The eighteenth century strongly inclined to a mechanical and atomistic view of things.   It borrowed its illustrations from physics and mathematics. It viewed language as an invention, not a growth.   It took Robinson Crusoe, the self-sufficient man on an island, as the unit of thought and feeling.   But the nineteenth century turned toward the organic realm for its conception of human method.[1]   And Hegel embodied this method to the full.   He even carried it to excess.   Humanity became too strong for men. He treated history largely as an affair of the idea. Individuals lost their footing.[2]   But the great gain was that the New Testament, being conceived as a human literature, was also conceived as a body, an organism, of thought and feeling, all its parts related both to one another and to the forces making through the great empire wherein they took shape.

Crisis of 1835.

The application of Hegelian principles to Bible-study brought about a crisis.   In the year 1835 appeared three books, all written by Hegelians.[3] The first was Vatke's *Old Testament Theology*.   It is mentioned here because it helped to indicate the tran-

---

[1] Paulsen, *Gesch. d. gelehrt. Unterrichts*, p. 513.

[2] Ranke, quoted in Lorenz, *Geschichtswissenschaft*, II, p. 58.

[3] Schwartz, *Gesch. d. Theologie*, pp. 3, 4 ; Pfleiderer, *Development of Theology*, p. 209.   For a qualification on the statement that Strauss and Baur were Hegelians, Baur, *Christ. Kirche*, V, p. 359, and Zeller, *Vorträge*, p. 401.   Zeller emphasises Baur's relation to Schleiermacher.   For an admirable sketch of the difference between Schleiermacher and Hegel, see Baur, *ib.*, pp. 350–355.   Yet the statement of the text is substantially sound.

sition of Hegelianism from the stage of philosophy to the stage of criticism, and also because it showed, through its treatment of the Old Testament as the record of a nation's religious experience, what the main consequence of the transition was to be. The second was Baur's treatise on the *Pastoral Epistles*. The third was Strauss's *Life of Jesus*, in its results and bearings the most significant book that has marked the course of Bible-study since 1750. Altogether, 1835 is something more than a date in the history of literature. It stands for a new turn and direction in the Higher Criticism.

The standpoint in the Hegelian view of revelation was the belief that no truth can be divine for man, unless it has been thought out within and appropriated by an integral human consciousness. From this position two diverging roads ran into the field of interpretation. A disciple of Hegel might emphasise the life of Christ as an objective thing which, while entering history through human feeling and thought, stood objectively before feeling and thought in order to be apprehended. In that case he might find himself somewhere near the position of orthodox Christianity. Or he might exclusively emphasise the subjective element in the New Testament, thinking of nothing but the process of human experience.

Strauss took the latter road. He was not spiritually interested in facts as such. Only the facts that are facts for and within the mind, touched him to the quick. He did not deal with a Christ who is a spiritual centre in an historic order of things. The only Christ he would have us know is the Christ within the Christian consciousness. His own Christianity, in the year 1835, was largely the philosophical product of his own genius. It was a great system of ideas resting upon his own reason as its base. So, very

Roads from Hegelianism into Bible-study.

Strauss.

naturally, he assumed that the Christ of the New Testament is, for the most part, the creation and product of the Christian consciousness. The question, How far is the Christ of the New Testament an historical figure? seemed to him a question foreign to the genius of Christianity. That there was a nucleus of historical reality he did not dream of denying. But to him it appeared to be relatively small. And whether it was large or small was an immaterial point. The sole essential thing, he said, is the fundamental law of our common nature and thought. This law, at work within the Christian consciousness upon the real or supposed facts in the life of Jesus, created the Christ of the New Testament.

Historical fact no part of religion.

Possibly, no more naïve book than the first edition of the *Life of Jesus* was ever written.[1] Strauss supposed, in good faith, that he was sacrificing only the accidents of Christianity. For, like the eighteenth century man, he assumed that historical fact can be no vital part of religion. He believed that his interpretation preserved the entire spiritual essence of Christianity. He declared that his method of exegesis was similar to Origen's. Allegory had been for ages the approved method of the Church. He was merely doing what the Church had done on a vast scale.[2]

Nemesis on the allegorical method.

In part, Strauss was right. Christianity has always rested, and will always rest, upon the historic facts of Scripture, — above all, upon the life of Christ. But the allegorical method of interpretation that dominated the Church for sixteen hundred years, obscured the historical foundations of Christianity by means of

---

[1] Strauss, *Leben Jesu*, 1835, I, p. vii: "Den inneren Kern des christlichen Glaubens weiss der Verfasser von seinen kritischen Untersuchungen völlig unabhängig"; Pfleiderer, *Development of Theology*, pp. 213–217.

[2] Strauss, *ib.*, I, pp. 6–51; Pfleiderer, *ib.*, pp. 213–215.

the vast dogmatic structure which was built up on the facts. For, as we have plainly seen, when once the doctrine of infallibility had preëmpted the Christian consciousness, it became necessary to slur over the simple historical sense of the Scriptures. Or, if it was not slurred over, it was looked upon as constituting a single element within a much larger body of thought. Now, as men interpret Christ's book, so will they interpret the Master himself. To obscure the sense of Scripture was, in effect, to overlay the cardinal facts of Christianity with philosophical and theological speculations. Hence, while nobody save Strauss could suppose that the total tendency of Strauss closely resembled that of Origen, the resemblance was close enough to explain an honest error.

By a slight stretch of words, Strauss might be called the *enfant terrible* of the allegorical system. The implicit assumption of the system is that the prime thing in Scripture is not the plain historical sense nor the original historical facts, but the spiritual ideas for which the facts stand as symbols. Now, this assumption disagrees with the Scriptural conception of revelation. In truth, it causes the Scriptures to Platonise. If it could have had its way in the Church, it would have substituted a splendid body of ideas for the saving facts of our religion. Of course, it could not have its way. Neither the powers of Hades nor the speculation of philosophers could remove the Church from her foundation. But in so far as the allegorical system did have its way, the true nature of revelation was clouded over. We may say, then, that Strauss let out the secret of the old exegetical methods. He was the divine nemesis upon a faulty and imperfect interpretation.

For, what he did, in distinction from what he thought he was doing, was to annihilate the very

Annihilation of Christianity.

being of Christianity. He made out the Christ to be
the creation of the Church. He undid the Biblical
idea of revelation. He volatilised the redemptive
deeds of God into a metaphysical system. And thus
he drove Christianity to its last, its one true line of
defences, — the original facts of revelation.

The ulti-
mate
question.

Protestant Christendom was now compelled to put
to itself the ultimate question. Criticism must go
down to the roots. The mental work of the Church,
in the period when the doctrine and limits of the
Canon were laid down, was credal and dogmatic.
The mental work of the Church in our period must
needs be, for the most part, critical and historical.
And to Strauss, more than to any other one man, we
owe the final clearing up of our ideas about the New
Testament. His challenge to Protestant Christians
was God's challenge to Christianity as a whole.

Life of
Christ fun-
damental.

The first main consequence was that the life of
Christ was seen to be the heart of Bible-study. The
churches had conceived the Bible too abstractly. The
connection between the book of Christ and the person
of Christ had not been sufficiently close and vital.[1]
But, after 1835, the life of the Saviour became the
fundamental question. Herein the work of Strauss
and the work of Schleiermacher joined consequences.
For Schleiermacher, before 1835, had proclaimed the
need which Strauss's work made so plain. The total
result was to make the person of Christ central.
Henceforward, the study of the historical life of our
Lord commanded attention precisely as the question
touching the Logos commanded it in the third and
fourth centuries.[2]

[1] Hagenbach, *Dogmengeschichte*, § 212, especially n. 1.

[2] Fairbairn, *Place of Christ in Modern Theology*. The study
of the life of Christ is a modern study. In the Nicene period
the Logos doctrine filled the mind. In the Middle Ages, the

The second main consequence was a more eager and
careful study of the Gospels, — the sources of our
knowledge regarding our Lord. Strauss himself did
not go deep into Gospel criticism.[1] He thought that
the Gospels abounded in unhistorical matter, — the
miracles in particular being plainly such. His object
was to remove all such matter from the original text.
Hence, his work was almost wholly a criticism of the
Gospel story. Only in a secondary sense was it Gospel criticism. But the direct result was that the
study of the Gospels entered a new stage.

In 1838 appeared Ullmann's book, *Historical or
Mythical.*[2] It was more dogmatic than critical. Its
aim was to prove that Christianity is unintelligible
save as the creation of Christ, and thus to cut the
ground from under the feet of Strauss. But it showed
clearly that the bearings of the latter's work were
immediately understood. Strauss was the thorn in
the flesh of evangelical Christians. Gospel criticism
became a matter of life and death.

In the same year came Weisse's *Evangelical History.*[3] The temper and method of the book, contrasted
with Eichhorn's hypothesis of an "Original Gospel"
(1804), show a decided change, though the change is
not all advance. But the emotional colour is livelier,
the religious interest is keener. Evidently, Gospel

life, so far as it was treated at all, was treated devotionally.
The eighteenth century, turning loose a free and destructive
doubt upon Christianity, made the study primary. Schleiermacher and Paulus anticipated Strauss in the name and conception of the discipline. But it was Strauss who forced the
churches to take the matter to heart. Upon the general stir
caused by Strauss, Baur, *Christ. Kirche,* V, pp. 379–382, and the
Studien Kritiken for the years 1835–1840.

[1] Zeller, *Strauss,* p. 41.

[2] Ullmann, *Historisch oder Mythisch,* 1838.

[3] Hermann Weisse, *Evangelische Geschichte,* 1838.

criticism has become a less literary, a more vital, matter. The cry, "to the sources," has taken a far more commanding tone.[1]

The philosophical mood dominated the higher thought of Germany down to 1830.[2] Strauss, passing over from that mood to the interpretation of the New Testament, carried with him a strong metaphysical bias. The results of his work were largely negative. He was a revolutionary, not a constructive, force.

Baur.

Baur took another road. His mind was indeed metaphysical in its bias, and his interests profoundly speculative.[3] His own words, "Without philosophy history is always, for me, dead and dumb," make a good text for a sketch of his life. Yet he differed broadly from Strauss. While philosophy was his inspiration in the study of history, none the less history was his end and aim. He was far more constructive than Strauss, his work more positive.

The divine without the human is nothing.

From Hegel's view of the divine and human life he drew his primary principle. He believed that nothing can have value for man or permanent significance for the historian, unless it has been worked out into life through a self-conscious, human process. Like his master, he despised the shallow illuminism of the

[1] Weisse and Wilke struck out about the same time the Mark hypothesis, which has since won so much favour that many of our contemporaries take it as a finality. Possibly some part of this air of finality is the product of weariness. Even scholars may be affected by the popular horror of mental suspense.

[2] Hegel died in 1831. Later, Schelling went to Berlin to preach a philosophical revival (Hase, *Kirchengeschichte*, 3ʳ Th., 2ᵉ abth. (1892), pp. 446–449). But, by the 40's, Germany's philosophical mood was on the wane, getting ready to pass into the study of the history of philosophy.

[3] Upon the periods of Baur's activity see *Realencycl.*; (1) "Philosophy of Religion," (2) "Biblical Criticism," (3) "Church History."

eighteenth century, which had no eyes save for the subjective aspects of things. The human is nothing without the divine. Illumination without revelation is blind. Thus, the idea of revelation recovers the dignity and honour it had lost. Yet it is equally true that the divine is nothing to us without the human. Revelation without illumination is empty. Therefore, it is not enough to say that the divine revelation recorded in the New Testament has a human aspect. If it is to be real for us, it must be conceived as a thorough and integral human movement. Neither is it enough to say that revelation has a history. It is a history.

Baur did not look upon the New Testament as being primarily a collection of books. He took the books as records of certain stages through which human life and thought — used by the divine life and mind as organ and instrument — had passed. So his controlling, coördinating conception was practically full-grown before he began his critical study. At least, it was so far ready within his mind that a very little critical work sufficed to call it forth. He could not take up the New Testament literature as single books. He took them in their unity, as mentally and spiritually related. It did not satisfy him, as it had satisfied Eichhorn, Schleiermacher, and De Wette, to settle the question of genuineness either for or against this or that document. Having proved, as he believed, that St. Paul could not have written "the so-called Pastoral Epistles," he went on to give them a definite place in the ecclesiastical history of the second century, a specific function in the mental economy of the Catholic Church.[1]

New Testament books constitute a unity.

---

[1] *Die sogenannte Pastoralbriefe*, 1835.

"Ich wenigstens vermag nicht einzusehen, wie die Frage, um welche es sich hier allein handeln kann, . . . anders entschie-

K

Baur's
dogmatism.

Beyond question, Baur's method was, to a considerable degree, dogmatic and high-handed. He was not truly critical. He did not first empty his mind of theory, then seek patiently for the facts; and, when he had found them, determine their full nature and scope, leaving the theory to ripen in the sunshine of assumed results. On the contrary, he had a philosophy of the New Testament history nearly complete within the first ten years of his New Testament study. He carried a sweeping hypothesis into the examination of the New Testament.

Jewish and
Pauline
Christianity.

In an essay upon the parties in the Corinthian Church [1] (1832), he had brought out the point that conflict played a large part in the movements of the Apostolic Church. Herein he took up and developed the suggestion of Semler and Paulus regarding the opposition between Jewish and Pauline Christianity. He thus started with a great fact, a fact that put to confusion the pious notion — seventeen hundred years old — that the Apostolic age was like the Saviour's garment, free from seams, a paradise of high-tempered peace. But he put his fact into the hands of the Hegelian formula for the interpretation of history. Hegel taught that all human development begins with a primitive synthesis wherein differences lie concealed, proceeds to an analysis wherein differences are brought to light, and ends with a deeper synthesis

---

den werden kann, als dadurch, dass wir sie mit den uns bekannten Erscheinungen innerhalb des ganzen Zeitraums, in welchen die Entstehung dieser Briefe fallen muss, also der Geschichte der beiden ersten Jahrhunderte, zusammenstellen," Vorrede. "Das Erste, auf was es bei einer kritischen Frage diese Art ankommt, ist unstreitig die auf bestimmte Data sich stützende *Totalanschauung*," etc. (the italics are mine). *Ib.*

[1] "Die Christus-partei in der Corinthgemeinde," in *Tübinger Zeitschrift*, 1832.

wherein the differences are unified. Working his data by the aid of this formula, Baur obtained a flowing outline of historical connection for all the New Testament books. Nothing was left at loose ends.

The unity that the New Testament had lost between 1750 and 1835 was thus regained. The dogmatic conception of the Canon put each document in its place. The books were held together by their common inspiration, their divine and mystical contents. When the dogmatic conception of the Canon fell into ruins, or serious disrepair, the books fell apart. They continued to be treated in connection with one another. But the reason for it was external rather than internal. And so long as that treatment lasted, the Higher Criticism failed to live up to its name. The "Lower" Criticism busies itself with the Text. The "Higher" Criticism undertakes to know the New Testament literature in an interior way. Baur began to pay in full the debt thus contracted. The New Testament books are seen to be closely coherent. They constitute an organism of thought and feeling. They have a magnificent human unity, through which the divine unity of idea manifests itself.

Literary unity replaces dogmatic unity.

The hypothesis left many facts out in the cold. Many others it put on the rack. It did violence to the nature of religion. It practically banished the supernatural. It was almost as much a dogmatic as it was a critical study. Baur was indeed one-sided: apparently, God never uses a smooth and rounded man to give a new turn to the world's thought. Yet criticism is under heavy obligations to him. We need not waste time in asking how far he was original, and how far he was the point where the forces of modern life, long gathering volume, came to a head. It does not matter whether he creatively marked out a path or merely represented a tendency. One thing is certain: New Testament study, since his time, has had a different colour.

Baur and Semler.

A comparison of Baur with Semler is instructive. For the latter was the pioneer of the movement from the Lower Criticism into the Higher, opening the history of criticism in the modern sense. And the former led the way into the period wherein we ourselves live.

Semler's treatment more dogmatic.

Semler, as we have seen, anticipated, in a vague fashion, Baur's starting-point, by distinguishing between the Jewish and Pauline elements of the New Testament. But he did not reach the conclusion by the same road. Baur, starting with a study of the Corinthian Church, came to his goal by way of investigation. Semler, a typical man of the eighteenth century, was possessed with the idea of an antipathy between the spiritual and the historical. The Judaising elements he considered accidental, chaff to be separated from the wheat of God's pure Word. The ancient conception of inspiration still controlled him. Baur, on the contrary, took the Judaising element of the New Testament to be an organic part of a spiritual total, a stadium through which Christianity passed on to a deeper understanding of itself. Semler's treatment was dogmatical; Baur's was historical.

Summary.

A rough but serviceable summary of the mental movement within the period of conscious criticism runs as follows. The treaty of Westphalia (1648) marks the end of the religious wars. Indifference and scepticism were now the order of the day. Deism became the bent and bias of the educated laity. The traditional theory of inspiration dissolved, and the Sacred Books came to close quarters with a self-reliant reason (1648-1750). Thus, the free study of the Canon became possible. But the old dogma ruled men from its burial urn. The cardinal, indeed the

sole, question was genuineness. New Testament study
was piecemeal (1750–1835). Finally, a great idea,
the idea of Humanity, laid hold of society with
destructive and renovating energy, gave a new birth
to poetry, took systematic form in philosophy, and
invaded the field of New Testament study. The
Sacred Books were treated as a spiritual total, the
product of and the witness to the supreme religious
revolution of history. And criticism, having been
for some time a floating conception, became a clear
ideal.[1]

---

[1] A more detailed summary of the stages in the critical movements from 1750 : —

(1) The ancient theory of Inspiration breaks down, leaving
the N. T. books open to free investigation. Semler's study of
the Canon is the type.

(2) The question of genuineness is the commanding one.
The N. T. books are studied as individual books. Schleiermacher on 1 Tim. and Luke's gospel (1817), Bretschneider on
the Fourth Gospel, Bleek on Hebrews (1828), are fine examples.

(3) The sweeping synthesis of Baur. N. T. scholarship takes
a different colour, in some respects a different temper. The
"totalanschauung" becomes the order of the day. *E.g.*
Schwegler, *Der Montanismus* (1841), Vorwort, p. iii.

Upon the general literary movement of Germany, with which
the critical movement is in touch, Schlosser, *Gesch. d. Achtzehnten Jahrh.* (1848), VII, 1ᵉ Abth., pp. 1, 2 ; Schmidt, *Gesch. d.
Deutschen Literatur seit Lessing's Tod* (4ᵉ Auf., 1858), III.

CHAPTER VIII

TENDENCIES [1]

The crisis. STRAUSS and Baur brought on a crisis. Up to their time, criticism had been a mental drift rather than a systematic programme. But, after 1835, an organised body of critical opinion took the field. In self-confidence it came near being a match for the dogmas that the eighteenth century cast off. Within the criticism lived and worked the Hegelian spirit, a spirit which, in all its forms, had a grand air of finality, and which gained, rather than lost, self-possession when it passed over into a theory of revelation.

The result was a violent precipitation. A new system of thought, a new programme of interpretation, if it be full of energy and the power of appeal, always works in that way. It is like a strong book. One is bound to agree strongly or to differ strongly. Either way, it clears the reader's head. Strenuous approval or strenuous resistance causes the perceptions that were previously vague to take shape and point. The reader arrives at a clearer knowledge of himself. Even so with an authoritative body of critical opinion,

[1] Literature: Pfleiderer, *Development of Theology*, Bk. 3, ch. 1 ; Watkins, *The Fourth Gospel* (Bampton Lectures, 1890), Lect. 5 ; Lichtenberger, *Hist. of German Theology in the Nineteenth Century*, tr. 1889 ; Hase, *Kirchengeschichte*, 3ʳ Th., 2ᵉ Abth. (1892); Zenos, *The Elements of the Higher Criticism* (1889), chs. 9 and 11.

such as that which followed 1835. Floating ideas precipitated themselves. Uneasy impressions hardened into convictions. Old views came forward with impassioned protest. New views took the air with prodigious self-enjoyment. Popular feeling was called in to settle academic questions. The man of the chair, stiffening under opposition, held his own opinions with deepening seriousness. Tendencies defined themselves. Men found their bearings.[1]

An enemy of the Higher Criticism might use the present state of religion in Germany as an indictment drawn up by history against the critical process. Here, he would truly say, is the home and hearth of criticism. And here, he would go on to say, religion is at a lower ebb than in any other Protestant country. In the university towns the academic body is largely hostile and indifferent. Amongst the people positive religion has a feeble hold. And this is the direct consequence of unrestrained, unbridled criticism. It has dried up the springs of religious devotion. It has dragged religious reverence from its old place of vantage. It has undermined religious habits. Opinion about the Bible is eager, fearless, and searching. And the Bible itself has largely lost its authority and power of appeal.

Criticism and state of religion in Germany.

No doubt, there is some truth in this statement of facts. When, however, we proceed to the analysis of causes, great caution is necessary. Other causes for the low ebb of religion in Protestant Germany may easily be suggested. One of them is the history of the social movement, into which a vast amount of

[1] There is a fine description of the way in which military conflict hardens and defines opinions in Moses Coit Tyler's *Literary History of the American Revolution*, 1897, Vol. I, opening pages. What he says holds true in greater or less degree of every severe crisis.

earnest thought and popular enthusiasm has gone. Nowhere else, save in France, has socialism come near being a religion in itself. And in France, the continuous existence and prestige of the Roman hierarchy on the one hand, the successive political revolutions on the other, have changed and deflected the current of social feeling. In Germany socialism has been, in effect, a religion. The political power being continuous and unimpaired, and the Church being so closely identified with the State that its pastors and teachers have been almost invariably hand in glove with the authorities, it has come to pass that Christianity is identified with opposition and indifference to the popular ideals.

Other causes lie close at hand. But no one of them concerns us, nor all of them together. A sober-minded Christian is not prone to think that he can see far into the mystery of the single soul. Still less will he presume to look deep into the mystery of a great nation's spiritual experience and say why one seed has grown and another has not. He knows that, in the economy of the Church universal, the Christians of any one given time are poor judges of the deepest consequences, the ultimate results of a great contemporary movement. What God may have in store for Germany, what new treasures of religious experience may some day be brought to light in the land of Luther — who but a child in the interpretation of history shall undertake to decide for or against?

New Testament treated historically.

The whole question is out of order. We are concerned with a certain great and commanding fact, — the story of the way in which the New Testament has come to be studied and valued as a history, — and with the reconstruction of the Christian conception of revelation which that study involves. We have seen how, after the fifth century, the Bible was taken farther and farther away from the field of common experience, the field where the layman's heart, the layman's reason, could find it and know it at first-hand. The keys of the deeper knowledge of the Bible were put into the hands of the monk and the Pope. The religious consciousness could not see the Word of God as it is in itself. Men must needs pass through Tradition in order to reach the sacred text; and, by the time they reached it, their minds were so filled with the Church's dogmas that they could not perceive the plainest and most outstanding objects.

If anything in the history of our religion is certain, this is certain; namely, that it is necessary to the true interpretation of the Scriptures, to the deep appreciation of God's Word, that Christians should go behind Tradition, should see the Sacred Books just as they were when they grew up within their time and place. If God has not willed that this should come to pass, then He has willed nothing. The establishment of the Catholic Church in the Roman Empire was certainly ordained by God. The free and fearless study of Holy Scripture was no less ordained by Him. Indeed, the one divine act drew the other after it. For the establishment of the Church involved the canonisation of the Scriptures. Their canonisation exalted their value far above all other literature. And this exaltation made criticism inevitable.

Free study of Scripture.

Great events need long periods to bring their deeper consequences to light. We must not presume to make our ignorance and our fears judges of the final result of the great work in which Germany has been the pioneer and leader. It is enough for us, who live only in the present and can see but parts of God's meaning and purposes, — it is enough for us to know that not without the divine will did Germany come to her task. Not for Germany alone, but for the world, has

Germany's work for the world.

the work been done. No doubt Germany has suffered
loss. Apparently, no great thing can ever come to
pass unless some damage attends it. But the loss in
this case has brought a harvest. If Germany has
undergone a decline in practical religion, her main
work has been well done. God assigns specific duties
to nations as to individuals. Can we doubt, when
once we have followed the course of criticism, can we
doubt that the Master of men assigned to Germany
the duty of free Bible-study? And if He has, it is
not our business to balance the books of universal history. Taking things as we find them, we must believe
that Germany's gain and loss have been for the whole
Church, to the end that the Word of God might be
unbound. If she has suffered, then her sufferings,
like the burning bodies of Latimer and Ridley, have
kindled a flame that cannot be put out.

No purely
critical
process is
possible.

It resulted, from the work of Strauss and Baur,
that criticism became a constructive principle, a definite programme. In a certain sense, it even became
an illusion. There has existed, these past sixty years,
a party of critics who have borne themselves as if
there were some such thing as a purely critical process, and as if they were its representatives. In truth,
there is no such thing as an absolutely pure critical
process. And the idolatrous estimate of the imaginary
standard of criticism is just another chapter in the
long history of the reign of words, another divorce
between words and things.

Criticism
not a body
of opinions.

We have learned that the causes which set criticism
on foot were many in number and diverse in nature;
and that the men of the chair unduly exalt themselves, if they suppose that the free study of the Bible
is a business which academic processes alone have
created, and which academic processes, by themselves,
maintain. The critics are part of a great stream of

interest and prejudice and passion. Criticism is a method, not a body of opinion. With it, as with science, the stake is not a certain conclusion, a particular set of truths, but truthfulness, the impassioned desire to find the original facts of sacred history. Now, dogmatic interest and points of view have been at work on all sides. The story of the purely dispassioned critic is another edition of Robinson Crusoe. And the ideal critic himself is not a fact, but a personification.

If the conceit of a purely critical process be kept up, it creates a new kind of orthodoxy. By the power of the keys which it confers, critics of this impossible class make bold to bind and loose. They put outside the critical pale those who retain any part of the supernatural interpretation of the origins of Christianity.[1] Criticism, however, is an ideal, not an accomplished fact. To identify it with any particular attitude toward any alleged fact is an act of usurpation. To get at the truth, the whole truth, and nothing but the truth, is the aim. To surrender all present views and connections, if they put themselves in the way of the search for truth, is the obligation. But, surely, it is at least conceivable that a mind strongly conservative might be more truly critical than the most radical critic, might have a holier desire to get at the whole body of facts recorded in the Scriptures. Nothing is to be gained by calling names or claiming titles. *Criticism an ideal.*

Facts that come from a world outside our deepest interests can be weighed without passion. Facts that *Entirely dispassionate criticism an impossibility.*

[1] *E.g.* Holzmann's treatment of Weiss and Beyschlag, *Einleitung*, 199. He assigns them to the " Dogmatisch Restauration " as distinguished from the " Wissenschaftliche Opposition." It requires a considerable dash of infallibility to draw the " scientific " line across the field of N. T. study in that fashion.

have little intrinsic weight may be assessed with a cool head. But Christianity is a fact at the very centre of Occidental history and as deep as life. It is not possible that the critic shall have an absolutely cool head, shall be altogether dispassioned. On all sides, deep feeling for or against some of the inherited beliefs of our religion is inevitable.

To organised Christianity, Strauss and Baur gave so grievous a wound that the most strenuous resistance followed. Christ is the estate and the endowment of Christianity. Our faith stands or falls with the person of its founder. From the beginning, it has built its claims to spiritual dominion upon the fact that in him deity and humanity fully met together. The rationalism of the eighteenth century reduced the supernatural events of the Gospels to purely natural occurrences. The philosophical criticism that came on the field in 1835 reduced them to symbolical, or representative, expressions of universal ideas. There were deep differences between Strauss and Baur. But their Christology had one fundamental quality in common: they translated the fact of the Incarnation, as Christians had understood it, into a personified idea.

General rally of forces.

That an interpretation like this should be widely or easily accepted on the spur of the moment, was out of the question. The critics who even dreamed of it — if any such there were — stood on the mental level of the men of the French Revolution who started a new calendar in 1792. Humanity has invested a vast amount of spiritual capital in the institutes of Christianity. The Church is so great a body, her roots are so deep in history, that she cannot easily be changed. In the nature of things, criticism of the kind that got vogue through Strauss and Baur, was the signal for a general rally of the forces of Protestant Germany.

The very standing-ground of Christianity seemed to be endangered. And when Baur's younger followers began to cut and slash the New Testament, it was as if a man should see the body of his dearest friend under the knife of a promising, but rough-handed, medical student. German Christianity had been shut in by God to the work of criticism. The task could not be avoided. The original text of revealed truth, the original elements of Scripture, must be seen in their native features and dress. But Christendom could not accept a dogmatic limitation of the scope and contents of the things that underpin and support it. The facts, and nothing but the facts, must be found and laid bare, no matter what befell the vested interests of the churches. What the facts were, however, in their whole scope and content, Baur and his followers could not be permitted to judge beforehand.

The challenge "To the sources!" must be accepted. The only alternative was to go back to the sheltering arms of Tradition — in other words, to enter the Roman Communion. And, in fact, a movement in that direction set in.[1] But it amounted to little. All the conditions that have given to Germany her intellectual leadership in the nineteenth century must be taken back before it could come to much. Protestantism was hedged in. The work of subjecting the Sacred Books to a searching examination was a divine and inevitable work. It did not follow, though, that the faith of Christendom in the supernatural elements

Defence of the supernatural elements in the New Testament.

---

[1] The "Romantic" movement (Haym, *Die romantische Schule*, 1870). Against "common sense" it exalted imagination and fancy. Against the eighteenth-century love of clearness it raised the mystical and the mysterious. And against the self-worship of the present and future it magnified the past. See also Omond, *The Romantic Triumph*, 1900.

of the New Testament was to be thrown overboard. On the contrary, they were sure to be strenuously defended.

1835-1850.

Everything combined to make the 30's and 40's a time of profound agitation.[1] German Christianity was stirred to the depths. On the one side, the old conception of the Bible, the old ideas of inspiration, the traditional methods of interpretation, reasserted themselves. On the other, the bold ideas, the aggressive methods, the sweeping claims of the new time let loose upon the old views a war that knew no quarter. Between these contending forces a great body of conservative Christian scholars, who believed that there could be no permanent conflict between the ideals of reason and the ideals of Scripture, sought to mediate.

Central points of critical opinion.

Two main points, kept carefully in mind, may enable us to get a clear view of the central elements in the masses of critical opinion that deployed on the field of New Testament study. One is given to us by Baur's interpretation of Apostolic history. He thought that Christianity started on its career as a Jewish sect.[2] Out of this provincial condition it was

---

[1] Political agitation. The Revolution of 1830 in France and the sympathetic movements in other countries ; the beginning of the socialistic movement which have so deeply affected the inner life of Germany. The growing prestige of the Roman Catholic Church in Germany ; Möhler's *Symbolik* (1832) was the herald of it (Baur, *Christ. Kirche*, V, pp. 309–320). The promulgation of the dogma of the Immaculate Conception of Mary (1854) betokened the deepened self-consciousness of the Papacy. Baur says truly regarding the general spirit of the time, " Charakter der neuesten Zeit, deren Tendenz es ist, die principiellen Gegensätze so viel möglich zu schärfen " (p. 309)

[2] One shrinks from so brief a description of a great scholar's views. To be absolutely clear one must leave out all colour and atmosphere, and so become somewhat unfair. It is true that

delivered by Paul. A bitter warfare between Jewish Christianity and Paulinism ensued. Finally, a Catholic Christianity, the Catholic Church and Canon, resulted from a deliberate compromise between the hostile parties. Within this framework Baur placed the New Testament literature. He found everywhere a tendency, a distinct dogmatic aim. And, in each case, the aim was defined by the relation of the individual author to the fundamental opposition between the original apostles and Paul.[1]

It is true that Baur's contribution to New Testament study would be most unfairly judged, if we summed it all up under this hypothesis.[2] His main work was positive and permanent. He set the example of treating the New Testament as an organic whole, a living body of literature to be understood only in connection with the turns and crises of an historical movement. He was the first to overcome the effects of the traditional, dogmatic conception of the Canon.

the "tendency" theory concerning the origin of our N. T. books was, for controversial purposes, the literary nerve of Baur's interpretation. Each book was assigned its position in time and space by reason of the conscious relation of its author to the supposed mortal conflict between the two wings of Apostolic Christianity. This was the salient point. Here the antithesis to the traditional view of the Canon massed its forces. Here, too, the idea of humanity took possession of the field and revolutionised the literary treatment of the N. T. Hence, in a brief history, it must needs have a practical monopoly of attention. But Baur's view of the first and second centuries was too large to be exhausted by a single hypothesis, however prominent it might be. His grasp of the period was wide and strong. His scholarship was prodigiously fertile. And not one of his many books was barren. For all his one-sidedness, he remains the greatest N. T. scholar within the past one hundred and fifty years.

[1] Baur, *Church History*, tr. 1878. One of the finest pieces of modern historical writing.

[2] Jülicher, *Einleitung i. d. N. T.*, 2ᵉ Aufl., 1894, p. 11.

But this part of his work was appropriated by everybody. It was a common gain. No one could put a private mark upon it. In this affair Baur represented and expressed the permanent mood of criticism. Consequently, we cannot use the attitude of scholars toward this conception as a guide to classification.

Paul and the Twelve.

The more strictly individual element in Baur's construction is the hypothesis of a mortal antipathy between St. Paul and the Twelve. And this will serve us well as a clew through the maze. The changing attitude of scholars toward this "tendency" theory gives us a fair indication of the degree to which the historical character of the New Testament has commended and approved itself to scholars since 1835. And seeing that our subject is the history of the way in which the New Testament has come to be interpreted as a history, we shall thus keep ourselves close to the subject in hand, while fitting ourselves to estimate the assured gains of criticism.

Person of Christ.

The other point to guide ourselves by is the personality of Jesus. "What think ye of Christ?" is the supreme question not only for the outsider who is looking toward the Church, but for the Church herself. Down to the eighteenth century, nobody doubted that Christ created Christianity. Christendom believed the Gospels to be solidly and literally historical. No one saw in them the work of the "later hand," or discovered the intrusion of evangelical legend and comment. Yet the Church, by her way of putting the supreme question, obscured both our Lord's humanity and the historical character of the books that attested his being and work, overlaying both with a thick deposit of dogma. The result was that, while the absolute historicity of the New Testament was assumed, the real answer was sought in the region of speculation, not in the field of Bible-study.

Strauss and Baur forced the Christian reason to put the question aright. We must go back of the great theological debate of the Nicene period. We must settle our accounts with the doubts touching the historical being and work of the Saviour. We must know him as he was on the earth, in his own words and deeds and sufferings. The historical Christ is the foundation of Christian theology. He must also be its touchstone.

This brings us to a point whence we may see that it is impossible to separate the critical from the theological movement. Back in the 30's and 40's there came a crisis in New Testament study. A little later, with the Neo-Kantian and Ritschlian developments, came an acute crisis in the history of theology. The two are parts of a common movement. This may serve to remind us once more of the cardinal fact that we are dealing with a history wherein "critical" motives and "dogmatic" motives are inextricably mingled. It may also help to press upon us the conviction that we should not expect to see deeply or clearly into a history of which we ourselves are so completely a part, and that we must leave to another age the task of passing a valuable and abiding judgment upon our own. *The critical and the theological movements.*

The crisis brought out the full force and thought of Germany. Individual influences formed schools of opinion. But deeper than these individual influences were the tendencies that sprang from the life of Christendom on the one hand, and the life of the age on the other. The tendencies are more significant than the schools. The latter stand for the common motives, the deliberate programmes of small bodies of scholars. For the most part, they are made by the tendencies. For no single scholar, however great and consecrated, and no set of scholars, however eager and devoted, *Tendencies more significant than schools.*

L

can do more than give a slight change of direction to the historical causes that issue from the collective and continuous life of the Christian world.   Only in part were the schools the places where men made up their minds.   Far more were they the places where men took observations, getting their bearings, and estimating the forces at work in the seething, tumultuous life about them.

Two main
tendencies.

Naturally, there were two main currents of feeling.   One of them came from the large and deepening experience of modern times.   Since the break-up of the mediæval world man has made two great discoveries, — the universe and his own past.   Nature and history have come upon reason with overpowering majesty.   The thought of the Greeks was chiefly philosophical.   The thought of the Nicene Age was almost wholly theological.   But the thought of our day is more and more exclusively scientific.   This is profoundly true even of Germany, where the one impressive philosophical movement of modern times ran its course.   Philosophy was a temporary, though a consuming, occupation of reason.   It was speedily followed by a passion for the study of nature and history.   Trendelenburg said that, in consequence of the Hegelian riot of metaphysics, Germany was like a man who, having drunk hard and long, waked out of his stupor with a splitting headache and feeling strongly disposed to take the pledge.[1]

Deepest
mood of
our time.

Compte's famous summary of the stages in experience is known to all.   Man begins his interpretation of his life and his world with theology, grows into metaphysics, and comes to maturity in science.   Taken as Compte meant it should be taken, — as the philosophy of history in a nutshell, — it is easy to find flaws

[1] Trendelenburg, *Logische Untersuchungen*, 2ᵈ ed., Vorwort.

in it. On the historical side, exceptions can be found with little difficulty. On the logical side, it is possible to show that the scientific stage of experience must give rise, sooner or later, to the old questions. But taken as a mental sign of the times, it is the most instructive generalisation of our century. For the intellectual mood and temper of our epoch is scientific beyond question. And equally beyond question this mood is bound to strengthen rather than weaken. For it is the mood begotten and fostered by the pressure on the mind of a vast body of unmeasured and unexplored facts. In the presence of the freshly discovered universe, and of all the matter included within the history of the human past, the scientific attitude is inevitable. The highest mental virtue of our time consists in the careful measurement of facts, in systematic experiment, and in a strong and unsleeping suspicion of dogmatic statements.

Now the Christian consciousness is not a little land of Goshen, whither the thought and feeling of the great outside world does not come. It is part and parcel of consciousness at large. That does not mean that Christianity is ruled by the world. The Head and Saviour of the Church has established his throne in the hearts of his people; he rules and renews them by influence from on high. But the Christian consciousness is in the world. Bible-study, then, cannot be a department of knowledge set off by itself. It must needs take a colour and bias from the general thought of the time.[1] *Bible-study and mental life of the time.*

The centre of our thought is the noble conception of law. And it has, apparently, a strong antipathy for *Idea of law.*

[1] This is saying nothing about modern Christianity which cannot be said about ancient Christianity. The Nicene Age took its mental categories and methods from Greek philosophy. Our age takes them from the scientific study of nature and history.

the idea of the supernatural. The supernatural seems to transgress by thrusting into history something tha refuses to relate itself to what goes before, thus making real history impossible.[1] Again, it seems to offend by letting down from above something that defies the law of cause and effect, and so claims the benefit of clergy when reason lays hands upon it, to examine and judge it. On both counts, the supernatural seems foreign to science and to a scientific interpretation of history.

Application to Bible-study.

That Bible-study, when it had once broken with Tradition and had carried the Sacred Books to the modern university to be examined, as all great objects are examined when they would have themselves taken seriously by modern men; that Bible-study should be profoundly affected by the ruling idea of law, was a matter of course. If it were not childish to balance the loss and gain in dealing with a matter that involves the inevitable, we might confidently say that the results, in the long run, are good. Just as our splendid conception of law provides the revelation of God's holy, creative Will with a logical apparatus proportional to its greatness, so the self-same conception renders the most loyal and efficient service to the study of revelation. For, as the Bible defines revelation, it is God's gift of Himself and His plan of salvation — the gift of saving unity and cleansing hopes — conveyed through the experience of men who met God in the ways of the common life. Revelation, therefore, not only has a history, but is a history. And since history is not rational, unless by law every part is related to every other part, it follows that our conception of law is the logical ally for which the Biblical idea of revelation has long waited.

---

[1] Strauss, tr. 1, pp. 1–4.

Nevertheless, when the great modern conception Criticism of
the history. came into the field of New Testament study, it brought in its train some companions of questionable origin and standing. An overpowering prepossession against the supernatural came with it. This led to a radical criticism of the evangelical history as distinguished from a criticism of the sources.[1] It was assumed, as a condition of New Testament study, that the supernatural elements in the life of our Lord were unhistorical. Now this assumption was not only in mental strife with the devotional mood of the Church; it was hostile to the mood of judicial criticism. Christianity is under bonds to know the facts touching its own origin in their proper shape, their pristine colour. But it cannot permit a so-called criticism to determine beforehand that all facts of a certain shape, all data of a certain colour, shall be condemned by a drumhead trial. This is not criticism, but dogma.

Strauss's method of dealing with the supernatural Strauss and
the super-
natural. was an advance upon that of the pious rationalism that characterised the period before him. Paulus took the Gospels practically in block, as the past handed them down to him. He then proceeded to translate the miraculous elements into the language of common sense. The supernatural kept its standing ground; the sacred text was undisturbed. The price paid, however, was ruinous. The method of Paulus was quite as vicious, exegetically, as the allegorical system of Origen. It violated the first principles of interpretation. The New Testament writers were not allowed to speak their own language. Far better, so far as the interests of the New Testament were con-

[1] Schwartz, *Gesch. d. Theol.*, pp. 146, 147 ; Ebrard, *The Gospel History* (tr. 1876), pp. 19–25 ; Zeller, *Strauss*, p. 41 ("The criticism . . . was not a criticism of the *Gospels*, but of the Gospel story").

cerned, was Strauss's frank dissolution of the supernatural into the legendary and mythical. Hereby the
fundamental principle of Protestantism — the obligation to discover the original text of the Scriptures,
the facts in their true order, the thoughts in their historical setting — was resolutely asserted. The Protestant Church could not, without self-stultification,
reject that principle. But neither could she, without
self-destruction, accept the dogmatic rejection of the
supernatural.

Conservative tendency. The other main tendency was the conservative. It
was not as strong nor as well intrenched as in Eng-
land. Had it been so, criticism would have run a very
different course. It is Germany's freedom of thought
and self-reliance of scholarly reason that has made
modern Bible-study possible. And these qualities do
not thrive in a very conservative climate. Yet, even
in Germany, the conservative forces were strong. The
Reformation was, first of all, a deed of the heart, an
impassioned insistence upon direct contact with the
Saviour.[1] Afterward it became a process of reason,
using the methods of the New Learning in order to
treat the Scriptures historically. Changed as were
many of the conditions in the nineteenth century, this
order of experience still held good. Criticism, as
an act of scattered individuals, was one thing. The
acceptance of the results of criticism by the great
body of Christians was another thing. The critical
process, considered at large, must subserve the emotional and spiritual needs of the Church.

Protestantism and Christ. Protestantism, from the very first, sought to commend itself as a defence of the honour of Christ. The
mediæval theory of the priesthood and of the Mass
had tended to make his part and function in the

[1] Hagenbach, *Dogmengeschichte*, § 211.

economy of the soul remote and passive. The mediæval theory of Tradition had done injury to the
sovereignty of his book. The Reformation was a
defence of his rights and honour. And fidelity to the
principles of the Reformation entailed the treatment
of the New Testament as a human literature; for
otherwise, the Saviour himself keeps remote from the
soul. His humanity is overcome by his deity. He
still remains an absentee from the interior affairs of
his Church. The Pope indeed is gone, his claims as
Vicar of Christ thrown into bankruptcy. But into his
place has come something nearly as bad, — a body of
fixed and infallible dogma. The Christ does not
transact his business with the soul at first-hand. His
honour is not secure.

The New Testament, then, must be humanised, or
all is lost. And when once it is humanised, the
abstract possibility of developments, of conflicts and
changes of view, of the growth of legend, of the unconscious alteration of original facts and colouring of
original words, must be frankly conceded. Otherwise, the Sacred Books are not human books. And
if they be not human, then the Saviour is not human,
and the spirit is gone out of religion. But Protestantism, for all that, even in the nineteenth century, is a
deed of the heart first, and afterward a deed of reason.
The Christian consciousness finds in the Saviour the
transcendent fact of the spiritual world. Through his
humanity it touches and sees the full being of deity.
It cannot, therefore, permit the critical process to
decide offhand that the supernatural elements in the
story of Christ are unhistorical aftergrowths. For
that would be tantamount to an admission that
humanity in its perfection must keep within range of
humanity on its average level. Dogma shall not shut
out searching criticism from the New Testament in

Legend in
the New
Testament.

the interest of orthodoxy.   But no more shall dogma
of another sort shut up our conception of our Lord's
humanity within bounds set either by science so-called
or philosophy so-called.   There shall be no abstract
criticism of the history, as distinct from the criticism
of the sources.

"Critical"
and "con-
servative"
not exclu-
sive of each
other.

These are the two main tendencies.   They cannot be fully classified by the terms "critical" and
"conservative."   It is true that a large amount of
dogmatic and irrational prejudice went into the conservative resistance to the free examination of the
New Testament literature.   Yet it is also true that a
very considerable amount of dogmatic prejudice against
the supernatural has gone along with the freer study
of the Sacred Books.   And, without stopping to weigh
and balance the one prejudice against the other, it
should be clear that the word "critical" is too broad
a term to be monopolised by those who, whatever
their scholarly merits, have completely broken with
the traditional conception of Christ.   Any form of
New Testament study is critical, exactly in so far as
it admits and affirms the necessity of bringing the
intellectual methods of our time to bear upon the
study of the Bible.   That is the only test.   A scholar
need not be uncritical, even if he has a very positive
faith in the supernatural.   Neither is he made critical by the most positive rejection of it.   We are concerned with a question of method, not with one or
another set of conclusions.   If, then, we speak of the
critical and the conservative tendencies, we must
remember that our words, though handy, are somewhat inexact, and must therefore be carefully watched.

CHAPTER IX

THE SCHOOLS

THE "schools" must be handled. And yet the treatment is not likely to be satisfactory.[2] In the first place, they are, at best, imperfect classifications. There are some names, of weight and consequence, that refuse to come within any group. In the second place, the groups lack in permanence. They are, at most, camps rather than schools — the temporary meeting grounds of men who are more or less of one mind. And even within each camp there are considerable differences of opinion and shifting relations. There are, then, grounds for serious dissatisfaction with the division of schools. Still, the division has its uses, particularly in a handbook whose limits, forbidding details, demand a sketch broadly done.

A common grouping has been "critical," "traditional," "mediating." What has been said under the head of "tendencies" is enough to show that the principle of division here used does violence to a true history of criticism. We cannot permit our master-word "critical" to be monopolised. Besides, this grouping has been done by men who would have little

"Critical," "traditional," "mediating."

[1] Literature : Zeller, "Die Tübinger historische Schule" (in *Vortäge*, I) ; Schaff, *Germany, its Universities*, etc. (1857); *Life of Schleiermacher* (tr. by Rowan); *Albrecht Ritschl*, by Otto Ritschl (2 vols., 1892–1896).

[2] Holtzmann considerably modifies it (*Einleitung*, pp. 186–207).

or nothing to do with the supernatural. In itself it is no less unfair than groupings made by men on the other side of the house. For example, Godet classifies New Testament scholars by their theological proclivities: they are "deistic" or "pantheistic" or "theistic." [1] The one principle of classification tacitly assumes that no man who believes in the supernatural can be truly critical. The other assumes that no man who rejects the supernatural can truly account for the existence and character of the New Testament books. Both assumptions are out of place. "Criticism" is an ideal common to all the earnest Bible-students of our time. The bond that unites them is the desire to see the facts and ideas of Scripture in their original order and connections. Classifications, which perpetuate theological and philosophical prejudices, though they may contain a certain truth, are a hindrance to the growth of mental sanity and charity.

The simpler the classification is, the nearer the approach to a bare designation of groups and scholars without any attempt at description, the less will it offend. To say little is sometimes the only way to say anything. We shall, therefore, give a brief summary of the positions taken (1) by the Tübingen School; (2) the believers in the correctness of the ancient traditions regarding the Sacred Books; (3) the school of Schleiermacher; and (4) the school of Ritschl.

Tübingen.   The Tübingen School is the school of Baur. It started with an overpowering emphasis upon the "tendencies" in the New Testament literature. The "tendency" interpretation becomes historically intelligible, if we set it against the conception of Scripture that prevailed from the fifth to the eighteenth cen-

[1] Godet, *Introduction to the N. T.* (tr. 1894), pp. 57-60.

tury. According to this, there was no process of human opinion in the New Testament. All the facts in the life of Christ and in the history of the Apostolic Church were accepted as original facts, with no element of legend anywhere about them. All the differences between the Gospels were taken as individual variations of a divine type, each variation perfect after its kind. The course of Apostolic history was absolutely clear and fixed, a series of divine events, as little dependent upon human motives and human struggles as the motions of the stars. Baur's interpretation made the New Testament the product of human thought and struggle. The primitive facts of Christ's life, the early years of Christianity, were differently valued, according to the point of view of the writer. Each author had a "tendency," a thesis to be established; and he used the data to prove his point.

The truth in the "tendency" theory has become a common gain of New Testament scholarship. We all know that the Gospels were not written as scientific biographies. They do not aim at completeness. Their narratives are sometimes divergent. Their reports of our Lord's words are sometimes coloured by the feeling of a later day. All this is permanent ground. But in Baur's statement of it, the "tendency" theory was closely akin, in its effects, to Strauss's mythical theory. The Jewish Christians shaped and coloured the facts in one way. The Paulinists shaped them in the opposite way. The Fusionists, or Catholics, who mediated between the extremes, still further slurred over the origins of Christianity, by making a compromise between two statements, each of which was largely unhistorical. Much the greater part of the New Testament fails us, when we ask direct questions touching the early situations and

"Tendency."

events. They afford us capital information regarding the moods of a later time. But when we ask them regarding the early times into which they project themselves, the information is indirect and secondary. Our view of those days must be built up almost wholly by inference and hypothesis.[1]

Baur's cashiering of the traditions.

Two main results followed. The first was the wholesale cashiering of the superscriptions of the New Testament books. Only four letters of Paul and the Apocalypse retained the authorship which antiquity assigned them. The latter is contemporary with the situations it describes, from the standpoint of Jewish Christianity. The Epistles to the Galatians, the Corinthians, and Romans are contemporary with the movements of mind and life which they record. All the other New Testament books come from times later than tradition had assigned them. They give us, not history, but highly coloured interpretations of history.

Person of Christ plays a small part.

The second result was that the person of Christ played a part but little greater than that of an occasioning cause. His creative relation to the new religion and the new community was neglected, although not dogmatically denied. Baur himself seemed to make Paul the true founder of Christianity as we know it. Some of his disciples went beyond him in this matter. They made a veritable gulf between Christianity as Jesus conceived it and lived it, and Christianity as Paul preached it.[2]

This did not lie in Baur's plan. Neither his philosophy nor his scholarship called for it. On the contrary, his Hegelian philosophy called for a conception of Jesus which should make him out to be the

[1] Fisher, *Supernatural Origin of Christianity;* Holtzmann, *Einleitung*, pp. 205, 206 ; Bleek-Mangold, *Einleitung*, p. 31 ; Schwartz, *Gesch. d. Theol.*, pp. 171–173.

[2] Bleek-Mangold, *Einleitung*, p. 49.

typical man, the one in whom the universal ideal was first realised. And his scholarship, using Paul as a vantage-ground for the reconstruction of the traditional views concerning Apostolic history, would have had to stand Paul on his head in order to avoid giving a true spiritual primacy to Jesus. Baur's earlier view was the natural one-sidedness of a path-breaker. At a later day he gave larger function and deeper significance to the person of Christ.[1] Yet he only went far enough to make plain the gap in the original theory. He did not bridge it.

Other members of the school have moderated Baur's principles and sobered his methods. They have, for the most part, abandoned his theory that Matthew is the earliest Gospel, taking up the Mark hypothesis, which, since Ebrard's time, has come to be accepted almost as a finality.[2] Hilgenfeld,[3] Holtzmann,[4] Weizsäcker,[5] Pfleiderer,[6] have practically abandoned the central point in Baur's position. They do not shut up the Twelve within a narrow "Jewish Christianity," but concede to them a real, albeit a provincial, catholicity. Now, this is equivalent to a surrender of a fundamental point in the "tendency" hypothesis. It drew after it the recognition that elements in the Gospels and in the Book of Acts, which Baur had assessed as products of a later dogmatic mood, are a genuine part of the primitive history. It also entailed a material shortening of the time required

Baur's principles moderated.

[1] *Vorlesungen über neutest. Theologie* (1864), pp. 75–121. In his earlier tendency to exalt Paul at the cost of Christ, Baur had forerunners (Reuss, *Hist. of N. T.*, I, pp. 53, 54).

[2] Hilgenfeld is the only considerable scholar who has held on to it. Badham, *St. Mark's Indebtedness to St. Matthew* (1897).

[3] Hilgenfeld, *Historisch-kritische Einleitung i. d. N. T.* (1875).

[4] Holtzmann, *Einleitung i. d. N. T.* (1886).

[5] Weizsäcker, *Apostolisches Zeitalter*, 2ᵉ Auf., 1892.

[6] Otto Pfleiderer, *Das Urchristenthum* (1887).

by Baur for the growth of the New Testament. The larger part of the New Testament is now found by most scholars within the bounds of the first century. Finally, some New Testament books that Baur classified as ungenuine have been accepted as genuine. This goes along with the change of base that resulted from the surrender of the original position of the school. If primitive Christianity was not the narrow sect Baur took it to be, and if the Twelve were not at swords' points with Paul, then there is room in an historical view of the early days for some things which Baur and his disciples excluded from it.

Thus the march of Baur's great hypothesis, being impeded by facts which it overstrained or dragged along against their will, and kept under the steady fire of facts which stood altogether outside the hypothesis, was slain at last in the house of its friends. But not until it had done what an hypothesis is designed to do. It stirred up discussion, inspired interest, and marked out the main lines of study.

"Fragment-ists."

On the side of method, the later members of the school became less sweeping. Compared with Baur they are "fragmentists."[1] This is due, on the one hand, to the decline of the dogmatic spirit that was so characteristic of the founder, and, on the other, to the recognition of the essential nature of a religious revolution like that recorded by the New Testament. It involves too many interests of human nature, it

[1] Harnack, *Chronologie d. altchrist. Literatur* (1897), pp. vii and ix. Two reasons might be advanced. (1) The growing prestige of science with the resulting suspicion of the "total-anschauung," of sweeping syntheses. (2) A decline in the theological passion that went into N. T. study back in the 30's and 40's. Whatever the cause, the result is not altogether bad. The "totalanschauung" is a good servant, but a poor master. It is not well for us to hear the grass growing in Palestine nineteen hundred years ago.

necessitates too many reconstructions of existing conceptions, too many readjustments of existing relations,
it is altogether too many-sided, to be taken within a
sweeping view. This intellectual "fragmentism" is
a welcome thing. The great constructive principle,
which Baur heralded, has done its full work in the
field of New Testament study. What is now needed
is patient and restrained study of the facts in detail.[1]

Protestantism, at its birth, received the traditional
information regarding the New Testament books at its
face value. Down to 1835 destructive doubt, while
it had touched and troubled this body of real or supposed knowledge, had not deeply wounded it. But
Baur dealt it a blow that seemed mortal. Hence the
conservative forces rallied eagerly to its defence.

Conservatism in Germany could not be what it has
been in England and America. There are two substantial differences in the situation. In England to
a marked degree, in America to a considerable degree,
the "Church" idea is strong. It is possible for men
outside as well as inside the Roman communion, by
leaning heavily with one arm on the principle of
authority, to get the other arm free for direct Bible-
study.[2] Whether this is a legitimate process or no,

Conserv-
atism in
Germany.

[1] In the matter of sweeping synthesis, Baur's mantle has
fallen upon the Dutch scholars, Pierson, Loman, etc. (Jülicher,
Einleitung, §§ 2, 8). Singularly enough, they stand Baur's
theory on its head, using the Book of Acts to prove the un-
genuineness of Galatians, etc. Sane scholarship is tempted to
wish that the rite of excommunication were within its control.
The only significant consequence of such criticism is to give
occasion to the enemies of criticism to settle themselves com-
fortably in the seat of the scornful.

[2] The book called *Lux Mundi* may be taken as partly coming
under this rule. Since the storm raised by *Essays and Reviews*,
the "High Churchmen" of the Anglican communion have found
it easier to change front than the "Low Churchmen." They have
used the "Church" to lessen the strain upon the Scriptures.

and how far the liberty thus acquired is real or permanent, are questions that do not here concern us. It is enough to know that on both sides of the water it is a possible procedure. The "Church" idea is now being used to take away the terrors of criticism, opening into popular acceptance a broad door for the selfsame critical process which a generation ago it forbade altogether.

The Church idea not strong.

In Protestant Germany the Church idea was not strong enough to play this part. It is true that a High Church movement went on, practically parallel with the Oxford Movement. The wave of romanticism that swept through Europe in the 20's and 30's carried a number of prominent individuals over to Rome. In alarm at this, and at the disintegrating tendencies of the day, an attempt was made to give to the Church a larger place, a more real authority.[1] This was in keeping with the political tendencies of the day. For, after Waterloo, the conservative forces of the State were in the saddle, and rode with a reckless hand.[2] Yet, with all this to favour, High Churchmanship made slight headway. The critical tendency was too strong to be roughly checked.

Academic thought aloof from popular feeling.

The other difference in the situation is found in that close connection between popular religious feeling and academic thought which is characteristic of England and America, and which has been notably absent from Germany. In the latter country the academic world has been a world almost by itself. The

---

[1] *E.g.* Kahnis (Kurz, *Church History* (tr. 1878), II, pp. 317, 373).

[2] Baur, *Christ. Kirche*, V, pp. 108–113 ; *Life of Schleiermacher*, II, p. 208. Hegel's glorification of the *status quo* — the monarchical appropriation of his principle, "the rational is the real," for use against the revolutionary and reformatory principle.

professor's chair is a long way from the pulpit.[1] So Biblical study, having its headquarters in the university, has been fearless and aggressive to a degree wholly beyond the reach of other Protestant lands.

Hence, the conservative wing of the critical movement had far less power either for attack or defence than it has with us. Yet it had considerable power. And in the early years of the reaction against Baur, it put forward a kind of scholarship that took a deep though insecure and troubled pleasure in the revival of the kind of knowledge that passed current after the fourth century. Thus Tischendorf, justly famous in the history of text-criticism, left his proper work to speak a word on the Higher Criticism that should bring controversy to an end. In his book entitled *When were the Gospels Written?* he went the whole length of the ancient tradition, asserting that the Apostle John closed and settled the New Testament Canon.[2] Thiersch, another apologete for the ancient traditions, accepted them in every detail, just as they passed over from the fourth century to the fifth. The New Testament Canon was practically constituted and bounded in the first century; and the doubts of the second and third centuries concerning certain books were due, not to uncertainty, but to extreme care and caution.[3] Guericke[4] and Wieseler[5] defended the tradition in a more moderate spirit than Tischendorf and Thiersch, yet on the same lines. Hoffman, head of the "Erlangen School," set up against Baur's central

Revival of purely traditional views.

---

[1] Reuss, *L'Église et l'École*, 1854.

[2] Tischendorf, *Wann wurden unsere Evangelien verfasst?* 2e Auf., 1865.

[3] Thiersch, *Versuch zur Herstellung d. histor. Standpunktes für die Kritik der neutest. Schriften*, 1845.

[4] Guericke, *Einleitung i. d. N. T.*, 1854.

[5] Wieseler, C. G., *Chronologie des apostol. Zeitalt.*, 1848.

M

thought a conception equally dogmatic. Baur carried
into the New Testament the Hegelian idea of development through contrariety; and where he could not find
a way for his conception he made one by main force.
Against this idea of development, Hoffmann set up
the thought of an organic unity of revelation unfold-
ing itself in divers ways at divers times. His conception was quite as true as Baur's, but, as he used it,
quite as arbitrary in its interference with history. It
always brought him, often by ingenious and winding
ways, into agreement with the traditions.[1]

Scholars
who be-
long to no
" School." Baur's central conception was opposed by othei
scholars, who differed widely from the group just
described. They cannot be called conservatives, being
altogether too free in their methods, too independent
of the traditions. They are mentioned at this point,
not because they belonged to any " School," but because,
chronologically, they come within Baur's own period.
Furthermore, they serve to remind us that we are
dealing with a vast movement, partly literary, partly
theological, partly religious. Naturally and inevitably, the crisis of 1835 called out every shade and
variety of opinion. We make use of the division into
schools not so much for the amount of ground it accu-
rately covers, as for the reason that, in dealing with
a vast literature, some sort of clew through the maze
is indispensable.

De Wette, in the fifth edition of his Introduction
(1847), set himself in opposition to Baur. His cool,
clear head guarded him from philosophical as well
as from dogmatic contagion. Ewald, a great scholar,
but a born fighter, vehemently assailed Baur's idea
of development through a fundamental antithesis

[1] Hoffmann, *Bleek-Mangold*, pp. 41, 42; Baur, *Christ. Kirche*,
pp. 411, 412.

between Petrinism and Paulinism.[1] Reuss, a true master in the Bible-work of our century, went his own way, independent both of Baur and the traditional view.   Unlike Ewald, he saw a truth in Baur's central conception, doing justice to the differences between Jewish Christianity and Paul.   At the same time, by his conception of Christ he made Christianity practically catholic from the beginning.   Hence, in his conclusions he found himself near most of the traditional positions.[2]

The school of Schleiermacher got the name of "mediating" because it sought, or seemed to seek, the middle ground between the critical and the conservative tendencies.[3]   Schleiermacher did not live to see the violent precipitation of opinion that followed 1835 († 1834).   He was altogether too many-sided a man to belong to any school.[4]   He was free in his

School of Schleiermacher.

---

[1] Ewald, *Die drei ersten Evangelien*, 1850 ; *Die Sendschreiben d. Ap. Paulus*, 1857 ; *Die Johan. Schriften*, 1861.   Work summed up in Vols. VI and VII of his *Volk Israel*.

[2] Reuss, *Histoire d. l. Theol. chrétienne*, etc., 1852–1864 ; *Gesch. d. heiligen Schrift N. T.*, 5th ed., 1874 (tr. 1884).   One of the best scholars of our century, singularly independent and cool-headed.

[3] The name " mediating school " is not wholly fair.   It suggests a conscious, almost self-conscious, attempt to find a *via media;* whereas the members of the "school" were, on the whole, as sincerely devoted to the truth, as the members of the "critical" school.   It is not worth the while of men outside Germany to perpetuate the *odium scholasticum* and *criticum* which has sometimes been strongly in evidence in Germany.

[4] "Es ist vielleicht nicht ein Theolog, welcher durchaus mit Schleiermacher übereinstimmt," says Gieseler in *Kirchengeschichte*, V, pp. 241, 242.   Hase well says that the Professor and the Pastor supplemented each other in him (*Kirchengeschichte*, p. 395), — something that cannot be said of many Germans. To those who would know the inner life of Germany it is as necessary to know Schleiermacher as to know Kant.

attitude toward the New Testament books.   Besides,
he affirmed the dogmatic insignificance of the Virgin
Birth and the bodily resurrection of our Lord.   Yet
the "mediating school" rightly claims him as its head.
For in Schleiermacher the two main needs of our century, the religious and the scientific, undertook to
settle their differences.   His heart was with the
Pietism of the eighteenth century.   And through his
heart he learned what Christianity is.   Christianity
is Christ — the historical Christ.   The one idea that
conveys permanent meaning to the Christian Church
is the idea that the ideal of the divine life does not
lie ahead, as a bare duty for the race, but lies behind
us and beneath us as an historical achievement.   The
divine life was perfectly realised in the human life
of Christ: realised within the human, not injuring
its integrity, doing no hurt to its rights.   This idea
is the everlasting content of the Christian consciousness, which has known from the beginning, without
a break, that Christ is its creator, and which finds in
the New Testament a trustworthy book of witness to
Christ's character and work.

In his thought, Schleiermacher was, in the fullest
sense, a man of our time.   He was all alive with
the passionate desire to know, to get at the original
forms of life and mind.   On the mental side he was
born a Greek, just as, on the emotional side, he was
born a Christian.   The religious and the scientific
moods mingled in him most deeply and subtly.   Possibly, he is the most representative man of our century.

Through the union of head and heart he worked out
of the fundamental heresy of the eighteenth century,
— its separation of the ideal and the historical.[1]   And,

Christianity and Christ.

Two elements in Schlei-ermacher.

[1] *Christ. Glaube* (1851), §§ 10, 11, 93 ; Nitzsch, *Evangel.
Dogmatik* (1892), p. 33 ; Reuss, *Hist. of the N. T.*, II, pp. 608,
609.

in principle, he had seen and overcome the main con- clusions of Strauss and Baur before they were broached. At the same time, by his mental strength and vigour, he opened wide the door into a fresh examination of the sources of our religion. Pietism and rationalism, even as they worked together in Semler, so they worked together in him, but after an incomparably deeper fashion. And so, when 1835 sounded the call to arms, the scholars who would fain pay in full the bond signed at the Reformation, took from Schleier- macher their text and their inspiration.

The funda- mental heresy of eighteenth century.

From this school came the Church historian, Nean- der. His famous saying, "The heart makes the theologian," expressed his point of view.[1] Easy as it is to distort and misapply the saying, none the less it contains a thought which has great weight, not merely for the theologian, but for the critic. The New Testament is, in the supreme sense, a book of religious feeling. Baur judged it from the standpoint of the speculative idea. As a result, not only did he misread many parts of it, he also mistook its spirit and method. For religious feeling does not communi- cate itself by speculation as the idea does, but chiefly by the contagion of enthusiasm. It is not an affair of the school; it is a popular movement. Its literary products do not smell of the lamp.[2] Its conclusions are reached not so much by logical processes as through the divining power of practical needs.[3] And it follows from this that a critic trained as Baur, and as many a critic since his day has been trained, in a purely philosophic and academic way, might be a poor judge

"The heart makes the theologian."

[1] Schaff, *Germany, Its Universities*, etc., p. 273 ; Baur, *Christ. Kirche*, p. 385.

[2] With the possible exception of the Ep. to the Hebrews.

[3] The practical line along which St. Paul works up to his great Christological position in Phil. 2. 1–6, is a good example.

— spite of strong analytic powers — of some things very material to a just and all-round view of the New Testament. Like to like is a good rule in interpretation. And it may fairly be doubted whether a critic whose knowledge of religion is well-nigh wholly literary and doctrinaire is likely to be a satisfactory judge of a book like the Fourth Gospel. Can a Russian understand the history of Magna Charta?[1]

Battle over the Fourth Gospel.

To gauge the work of the school of Schleiermacher, the Tübingen school must be kept in mind. Baur's great hypothesis was either the point of view or the point of attack for all the New Testament scholars. The so-called "tendency" theory, the position that the historical books of the New Testament are not so much historical as dogmatic, was naturally the chief offence to those who stood anywhere near the traditional view of Christianity. And inasmuch as the Fourth Gospel was assessed by Baur as the extreme case of "tendency," — it being, in fact, a theological romance, — around it the fiercest fighting raged. Indeed, without going far astray, one might take the history of the Johannine question as a vertical cut through the entire history of New Testament study since its turning-point.[2]

Members of school.

Bleek († 1859) was a devoted pupil of Schleiermacher, and his master said of him that he had the charism of "Introduction," of historical insight into the problems and connections of Biblical study.[3] The word was

---

[1] Compare Freeman, *Methods of Historical Study* (1886), p. 289.

[2] Watkins, *Fourth Gospel*.

[3] Bleek, *Introduction to N. T.* (tr. 1879). In his mental quality he resembled Bretschneider, De Wette, and other scholars of an earlier period, who were content oftentimes to reach a probability (K. J. Nitzsch in *Realencycl.* (1897), p. 256). "Probability" went out of fashion when Baur came in.

well said. For Bleek is one of the sanest and sound-
est scholars of our century. He defended the Fourth
Gospel with special zeal. He adhered to the traditions
concerning the New Testament Canon almost in block.
Yet he was fair-minded to a high degree. Lechler,
unlike Bleek, whose Biblical studies were well
advanced before Baur came above the horizon, was
conceived, and born, and bred in mental opposition to
the Tübingen school. Hence, perhaps, a certain mental impetuosity, which he shared with the scholars of
his time. Baur introduced hypotheses of the grand
style into New Testament studies, and made them the
order of the day for his friends and foes alike.
Lechler accepts from Baur the idea that the Pauline
doctrine is the dominating point in the Apostolic
age; but finds in it nothing but a clear expression of
the teaching of the Twelve. By the help of this conception, he achieves a view of Apostolic development
which keeps close to the traditional lines; at the same
time, he is hardly inferior to Baur in the art of hearing grass grow in the Holy Land.[1] More recently,
Weiss has used a conception practically identical with
Lechler's, but with a far larger fund of exact knowledge and with a better-balanced judgment.[2]

The school of Ritschl succeeded the school of
Schleiermacher in theology, and, in some measure, in
criticism. Its founder began his career in the school
of Baur.[3] From it he got his start, learning how to
put the main question. Down to the Reformation, as
we have seen, the Church and the Bible were treated
as inseparable parts of one mystical body of truth —
the whole of it lifted above the level of reason, beyond

School of
Ritschl.

---

[1] Lechler, *Apostolic and Post-Apostolic Times*, 1851, tr. 1886.
[2] Bernhard Weiss, *Einleitung i. d. N. T.*, 2ᵉ Auf., 1889.
[3] Bleek-Mangold, pp. 51, 52 ; Ritschl's *Leben*.

the reach of questions, and, consequently, put out of touch with history. The Reformation tore the idea of the Church away from the idea of Scripture and threw it to reason to be investigated and discussed. But **Relation of Church and Bible.** the Bible still held its head high above reason and history. The eighteenth century broke down its guard, by decomposing the ancient conception of inspiration. For a while the study of the Canon was pursued along literary lines. Then Baur led the way into the study of the New Testament as the record and product of an historical movement. And now the ideas of the Church and Bible, long separated, came together again. It is seen that the Church and the Canon grew up together. Baur, overusing the fact of strife within the Apostolic Church and staying himself upon certain phenomena of the second century,[1] derived the origin of the Church from the impassioned Judaism of the Twelve. Hence, in order to account for our existing New Testament, — it being almost wholly non-Jewish and Catholic, — he needed a long course of years after the fall of Jerusalem in the year 70.

" Origin of Old Catholic Church." Ritschl learned from Baur how to put the question. In 1850 he published a book entitled *The Origin of the Old Catholic Church.*[2] The title is luminous. If we would understand the rise of our New Testament Scriptures, we must understand the rise of the Old Catholic Church, or the Church of the second century. In the second edition of his book (1857) Ritschl broke completely away from Baur's explanation.[3] The Christianity of the second century resulted from the popularisation of Paulinism. Paulinism, therefore,

[1] Estimate of Pseudo-Clementine literature in *Church History of First Three Centuries.*

[2] Ritschl, *Die Entstehung der altkatholischen Kirche*, 1850.

[3] Ritschl had precursors (*Bleek-Mangold*, pp. 46, 47).

not Judaism, was the real foundation of the Old Catholic Church. Herewith Baur's hypothesis was hit in a vital part. The "tendency" idea henceforward fluttered away with a wounded wing. For, however marked the differences between Paul and the Twelve, they are substantially one.

Reuss said, in criticism of Baur's theory, that developments may be parallel; that they are not necessarily successive. The point of the saying is here; a great religious and social revolution is inevitably many-sided. Baur ended by putting the New Testament literature on the rack, in order to force it into conformity with a rigid conception of development.[1] But life is infinitely larger than logic, and the Christian life of the first century will not support Baur's interpretation of its literature. Ritschl, starting as a member of the Tübingen school, as free as Baur himself from "entangling alliances" with the traditional scheme of knowledge about the New Testament books, attacked the great hypothesis upon purely historical grounds. He so far overcame it that substantial modifications became necessary, if the hypothesis was to retain any scholarly standing.

Life and logic.

This much secured, equally substantial modifications of Baur's chronology of New Testament literature must follow. Harnack's declarations regarding the Tübingen school are, possibly, a trifle sweeping.[2] His affirmation that the chronologic framework within which the traditions placed the New Testament books is correct in nearly every particular, has, perhaps, too imposing an air of finality.[3] But he is within bounds

Modification of Tübingen chronology.

[1] Cf. Hegel's handling of the history of philosophy (Zeller, *Philosophie der Griechen* (4e Auf., 1876), I, pp. 8–11).

[2] *Chronologie*, etc., p. ix. Holtzmann's criticism is essentially just (*Einleitung*, pp. 205–207).

[3] *Chronologie*, p. x. The cries of joy with which England

when he affirms that the relative mental and spiritual unity of the New Testament would not have been possible, had not its various books been written within a comparatively short period.   This "was the Achilles' heel in Baur's construction of Apostolic history." [1]

and America saluted Harnack's proclamation gave melancholy proof of the nervous condition of the Churches.

[1] Bruno Bauer and Feuerbach are men whom it is impossible to group under any of the heads used above, without doing serious injustice to their neighbours.   Taken together, however, they constitute a phenomenon of which our subject must take serious account.   They are a notable mental symptom.   In both of them the human swallowed the divine.   "Anthropology is the secret of theology," was Feuerbach's text.   Jesus and Paul are dramatic creations, was Bruno Bauer's thesis.   As indicating a current of feeling deep and strong in our day, they are significant.   Cf. Feuerbach with Comte.   Höffding, *Hist. of Modern Philosophy* (tr. 1890), II, pp. 272–293 ; Baur, *Christ. Kirche*, pp. 390–394 ; Schmidt, *Gesch. d. deutschen Lit.*, III, pp. 271–290.

CHAPTER X

THE one solid and certain gain of criticism is that the study of the New Testament has entered, once for all, the historical stage. Other things are in doubt. Touching the specific questions broached since 1750, it is not safe or wise to say that we have got down to the bottom facts. We have shaped no final judgments. Our most assured results do not rise higher than a very strong probability. One thing, however, is secure. The Sacred Books are being studied as thoroughly human books. And they are being studied in the historical spirit.

The historical spirit the chief gain.

The sense of fact has triumphed over the dogma of infallibility in all its forms. It was impossible, as long as that dogma held its ground, for the original facts of sacred history, the original thought and feeling of the men of the Bible, to come into view. Infallibility, whether Biblical or ecclesiastical, is an arrangement whereby the definitions of a later time, assuming a fictitious finality, draw upon the credit of a sacred past to pay their debts to reason. The Sacred Books were indeed exalted on high. No man dared question them. They were above examination. The

Sense of fact and dogma of infallibility.

[1] Droysen, *Principles of History*, tr. by Andrews; Gervinus, *Grundzüge der Historik*, 1837 ; Briggs, *The Study of the Holy Scriptures*, 1899; Baur, F. C., *Die Epochen d. kirchlichen Geschichtschreibung*, 1852 ; Freeman, *Methods of Historical Study*, 1886 ; Bernheim, *Handbuch d. histor. Methode*.

devout student of the ancient days said, regarding them, that they were like a great river, on whose edge the little child may play, and in whose depths the elephant, the mightiest of living creatures, loses his footing. And he spoke the truth. For the Scriptures, the books of witness to the saving unity of the divine life, are level with the highest human praise.

But the Scriptures paid a heavy price for their alleged infallibility. They were insured against fearless reason, against scientific curiosity. From what source, though, issued the insurance? Not from themselves. In the last resort, it came from the infallibility of the Church. And so, in order to find a safe asylum, the Bible must hand over the keys of interpretation to a monasticised, clerical establishment heading up in a Pope. By so doing, however, the Bible disowns its own history. Monks and mystics did not write it. And all the monks and mystics put together cannot find the heart of its mystery. The Bible, to be rightly interpreted, must have the power of the keys in its own hands. It will not pay the price which the attribute of infallibility demands. It prefers to be examined, to be questioned, to take its chances with a fearless reason.

Outlying. facts.

Now, the essence of reason is the imperative and authoritative feeling of outlying facts. In the form of psychology reason deals with the processes of mind. In the form of science it deals with the universe besetting the mind. In the form of philosophy it deals with the final questions to which experience, taken largely, gives rise. But in every form reason, if it be lively and forthputting, consists in an imperative sense of facts lying out beyond the received and established explanations, and in the feeling of authoritative obligation to know the facts as they are in themselves. Consequently, the dogma of infallibility, if it be anything more than a legal fiction or a pious epithet, if it be taken seriously, is foreign to reason. By ascribing an unnatural and impossible finality to established interpretations, it keeps the outlying facts of revelation from exercising due pressure upon the mind of the Church. At the same time, it is foreign to the character of revelation; for, when followed home, it turns the human author of the Sacred Books out of doors, leaving the Divine Author in exclusive possession. So reason and the Bible have conspired to make the sense of fact supreme over the dogmatic needs of the Church establishment.

Reason and revelation both opposed to infallibility.

This is our great and permanent gain. It cannot be taken away from us. The conditions of the time safeguard it.[1] The scientific motive and the religious motive are united in their devotion to this end. The historical spirit, in New Testament study, the spirit whose sole concern is the being and scope of the original facts and thought of Apostolic history, — the original text of our Lord's life and words, — has taken the sceptre and cannot be dethroned. The New Testament books are no longer to be studied in the dogmatic mood.[2]

[1] The contrast between our age and that wherein the principle of Tradition found a free field is as broad as it can well be. Our commerce is vast. The race is throwing all its accumulations of experience into one collection. Ideas and impressions are in eager competition. The study of religion is comparative. The body of facts within our ken is steadily and rapidly growing, and every increase of data deepens our feeling for the facts that are pressing forward into knowledge. Reason is forced to keep open house. Hypotheses cannot maintain a fixed form.

[2] The work of Robinson might be taken as typical. He sought to strip off the false skin of " topographical tradition long since fastened upon the Holy Land by foreign ecclesiastics and monks " (*Biblical Researches*, 1841, I, pp. vii, viii). In just the same way criticism has stripped from the N. T. books the false skin of ecclesiastical tradition and theory fastened upon them by a later time.

Idea of de-
velopment.

The idea of evolution has come in the train of the historical spirit.[1] The need of it was not nearly so great in the field of the New Testament as it was in the field of the Old. There are considerable elements in the Old Testament which belong to early and out-grown stages of religious experience. The Fathers, wholly lacking our idea, could not make their presence in Scripture intelligible save by the help of the allegorical interpretation. Without allegory they must needs have rejected the divine authorship of the Old Testament. Evolution makes allegory needless. The things which so greatly troubled the Fathers become for us intelligible as parts of the divine schooling of Israel.

No such need ever existed in New Testament study; for the New Testament contains no Levitical and primitive elements. None the less, when we consider the matter more from a general and less from a specific point of view, the profits of the New Testament are as great as those of the Old. There is a mental movement and change amongst the men of the New Testament. But under the old categories or habits of thought, change was irreconcilable with the divine. The divine, as such, was always conceived to be immutable. Hence, the divine self-revelation could not realise itself in a truly historical way: for history necessarily involves change.

Ancient in-
terpretation
lacked it.

The history of heresy makes some strange bedfellows. The fundamental error of the eighteenth century was its disbelief in the capacity of the historical

---

[1] The idea of evolution, like the true conception of language and grammar, took shape outside the field of Biblical study. Yet the Biblical doctrine of the Kingdom of God is one of the main causes of the conception ; for evolution was a social programme before it became a scientific hypothesis. The idea is not a trespasser upon the Biblical field.

to take in the ideal, and in the ability or disposition of the ideal to possess and pervade the historical. This error tinged all thought regarding revelation. Kant's view was as deeply discoloured by it as Tom Paine's. Now, so far as the forms of thought go, this root-error is identical with the implicit premise of the ancient Church. If we were to classify theologians by the way in which their minds work, rather than by the specific forms which their theological systems assume and the objects of devotion on which their minds rest, we might discover that the deistic thought of the eighteenth century has an alarming family likeness to patristic orthodoxy. For the latter is no more able than the former to think together the idea of a divine revelation and the conception of a genuine historical movement.

Practically, the Bible-students of ancient times were forced to choose between the idea of revelation and the idea of history. Now, devout men, when driven to a choice like that, will not hesitate for a moment. They will sacrifice the history in order to save the revelation. So with the Fathers. They did not purposely belittle, far less reject, the historical. Origen must needs have gone mad before he could consciously lower the significance of the historical and human Saviour. But the simple truth is, that they could not, with all the good intentions in the world, keep themselves true to that conception of revelation which the Bible itself contains. The mental life of antiquity gave them no help toward overcoming the apparent antipathy between the ideal and the historical. On the contrary, the thought-forms of the period fostered the difficulty.[1] Against its will, the Bible-

---

[1] Aristotle, seeking to correct the one-sidedness of Plato's idealism and so build a bridge from " being " to " becoming," struck out the theory of evolution. It is the supreme evidence

study of antiquity caused revelation and history to spring apart.

History and revelation could not be made to square.

By the help of the idea of evolution revelation and history become congenial. For the conception of being and the fact of change are reconciled. In antiquity they could not meet. So the worthful, the divine, was identified with the unchangeable. But in the modern view the worthful and the changeable are organic to each other; we cannot conceive of a law that does not express itself in movement and growth. So we are enabled, by the mental habits of the time, to drive the old heresy out of consciousness. To our thinking, revelation is so far from being suspicious of history that it demands it. Thus the Divine Author of Scripture takes the human author to be his prophet and interpreter.[1]

The idea of development brings them together.

The reign of allegory is ended. The patristic Bible-student could not get out from under its power. He could not think of the changeable except as the profane and unworthful. Only the unchanging could be divine. And so he conceived the Scriptures as all of one piece from Genesis to the Apocalypse, as being one solid block of inspired truth. What he found in any part of the Bible, he could find in all parts.

---

of his genius. But Aristotle was ages ahead of his time. Greek thought, taken in bulk, was far from helping the Christian consciousness to reconcile the ideal and the historical. It was in truth a severe handicap. Greek speculation as a body cared almost nothing for history.

[1] The belief in evolution has become the personal equation of our day. Hence the student needs to be on guard against it; for if one looks long enough, one always finds what one expects to find. In the contemporary knowledge of the N. T. there is a considerable surplusage which the facts never suggested and which they will not sustain. The chief part of it is the product of new-fangled "psychology" on the one hand and an overworked idea of evolution on the other.

The deepest truths of the New Testament stood out everywhere in the Old. The Old was level with the New. But to bring it level, no way would serve, except the way of allegory. As long as men thought of the divine as the absolutely unchangeable, there was no other road to take. Now, we have seen that the allegorical principle, once adopted, would have let loose a chaos of interpretations, unless a dogmatic tradition had bridled it. But the dogmatic tradition, to be efficient, required a great clerical establishment to work it. Then this establishment, to make the sacred text give answers that squared with its needs, had to use the allegorical method which it had undertaken to bridle. So the allegorical principle remained in full force.

The modern student, thanks to the historical spirit and to the great conception that comes in its train, rids himself of allegory, without doing injury to the divine character of Scripture. If he be as reverent as he is critical, he will do the kind of work that the great scholars of the ancient Church would have rejoiced to do, had the mental apparatus of their times permitted it. He is giving the Bible the highest possible honour. Through his labours, the sacred text has come at last to its rights. It is being studied and known as it is in itself, and interpreted along the interior lines of its own meaning and purpose.

Allegorical principle finally overcome.

The historical spirit has registered its results under various departments, or "disciplines." Each of them, in its own way, pays tribute to the new ideal of New Testament study. For example, "Introduction." As to its scope, opinions differ. But there is no difference as to its aim and method. It is historical; that is, it undertakes to set the Sacred Books within the frame of their time and place. There has been some dispute in Germany touching the claims of one

N

and another scholar upon the title to the first use of the conception.[1]   The dispute is not altogether becoming to the dignity of scholarship.   The conception of Introduction as historical was the product of the time rather than the work of any individual. The word needed only to be spoken, in order to be universally approved.   Indeed, it has become so much a matter of course that, possibly, we shall drop the adjective "historical" in the title of our Introductions.[2]   The aim of our Introduction is instinctively non-dogmatic.   It has no traditions to drill into the student.   Its one purpose is to find the New Testament books at home within the circumstances that caused their conception and occasioned their birth.[3]

Again, the theology of the New Testament marks the triumph of the historical over the dogmatic spirit. From the date of Origen's treatise on theology down to the eighteenth century, systematic divinity was universally assumed to be one and the selfsame thing with the theology of the Scriptures.   This was inevitable.   Just as long as a dogmatic tradition, taking itself in good faith as infallible, filled and ruled the whole mind of the Church, it was impossible for the idea of a material difference between the established opinion of the day and the thought of the Scripture to find entrance.   But when Tradition broke down and dogmatic divinity lost standing before

---

[1] Credner (1836), Hupfeld (*Ueber Begriff u. Methode der sog. bib. Einl.*, 1844), Bleek (*Introduction*, I, p. 1 ; *Bleek-Mangold*, p. 5), and Reuss have claims upon it.

[2] Weiss, *Einleitung i. d. N. T.*, p. 19, n. 1 ; Reuss, *Hist. of N. T.*, I, pp. 1, 2.

[3] If the student will read what Cassiodorus has to say about the N. T. books, and then, at the same sitting, read some modern primer like Bennett's *Primer of the Bible* or Dodd's *Introduction*, he will realise how broad is the gulf between the sixth century and our own.

reason, men were enabled to entertain the idea that the theology of the men of the Bible must be understood and stated as if the theology of Tradition had never been dreamed of.[1]

So, too, the form of study entitled "The Apostolic Age" has humanised the ancient conception of the Canon. That conception, after the fourth century, brought the New Testament before the mind's eye as a mystical total, with no suggestion of movement or change, the light of the divine so flooding it that the light of the human was obliterated even as the sun in his strength obliterates the stars. But "the Apostolic Age" brings the New Testament literature before us as the outgrowth of and the witness to a life that was rich in human expression and sympathised with great historical movements.

"The Apostolic Age."

And so, in every way, the stage of New Testament study, into which we have entered, is inspired, if not dominated, by the historical spirit. And as the total result, that past which for the Christian Church is the sacred and authoritative past, — the person and mind of Christ, the experience and interpretation of the Apostles, — is rising before our eyes in its proper shape and its pristine beauty. The debt of Christianity to Christ, that debt which the Nicene Church contracted, the mediæval Church postponed, and the Reformation Church promised to pay, is being paid. We are seeking to know our Lord according to his own mind.

Christianity paying its debt to Christ.

[1] The Reformation, in its earliest days, pledged Christianity to this study. Luther's wrath against metaphysics. Calvin's purpose to correct theology by sound Bible-study ("Jean Calvin au Lecteur," preface to *Institution de la Religion Chrestienne*, 1560). But the pledge did not begin to be kept until the eighteenth century.

CHAPTER XI

THE INSPIRATION OF CRITICISM [1]

THE history of the interpretation of the New Testament has two periods. The first is the credal or
dogmatic period, stretching from the year 200 [2] —
when, speaking roughly, the Christian Bible was
formed by binding the New Testament books into one
body with the Old Testament — to the Reformation.
In the early part of this period, a splendid system of
theology was shaped, the doctrine of Tradition took
form, and the Creeds became the mental constitution
of the Church. In the later part, Tradition found a
free field for its development. The conception of infallibility, the stress of the times, the triumph of the
Papacy, conspired to drive a certain view of inspiration, a certain set of opinions about the Sacred Books,
deep into the Christian consciousness — apparently,
almost as deep as life. Meanwhile, Biblical study
had created a vast literature. Indeed, to comment on
Holy Scripture was the most serious occupation of
high-minded men. But the study was altogether dogmatic and devotional. The established opinions about

[1] Fairbairn, *The Place of Christ in Modern Theology;*
Cheyne, *The Hallowing of Criticism;* Seebohm, Colet (in
Oxford Reformers, 3d ed.); Fichte, *Ideal of a Scholar;* Salmon,
Infallibility; Reuss, *Hist. of the Canon of the Holy Scriptures*,
2d ed., tr. 1891 (especially the last chapter, entitled " Criticism
and the Church ").

[2] Harnack, *Das N. T. um d. J. 200*, 1889.

the Bible were accepted as final. It entered no man's thought to suggest that the facts of Scripture were at odds with Tradition. No one dreamed that it was necessary to go behind Tradition, in order to find the Word of God.

The second period reaches from the Reformation to our own day. The Protestants of the sixteenth and seventeenth centuries were, for the most part, no less dogmatic than the mediæval scholars. But by setting the idea of an infallible Bible at swords' points with the idea of an infallible Church, they effectually shattered the unity and authority of Tradition. The Bible came into direct contact with consciousness. The critical principle was established. It was only a question of time when the Scriptures must speak for themselves. And time did not tarry. The eighteenth century, the hinge in the history of interpretation, threw theology and Tradition into bankruptcy. A new kind of authority appeared, the authority of facts, — the facts of Nature and the facts of history. To see things as they are in themselves, without regard to inherited opinions about things, became a supreme mental obligation. The entire mental process, no matter what the object on which the mind acted, became critical.

Reformation — our own time.

The Bible, having broken away from the protection and imprisonment of Tradition, must needs submit itself to fearless, first-hand study. The Church authority which, in the thirteenth century, had said to reason, "Thus far but no farther!" no longer stood on guard. The Bible, speaking for itself, must speak to reason. Bible-study becomes direct. Criticism is the order of the day. It enters, as a new ideal, into the life of the Church.

First-hand study and knowledge.

Those words are not strained. By an ideal we mean a vision of life that sets us upon a journey, through

Criticism a new ideal.

duty, into a promised land of peace and power. And, in all soberness, unless the direct or critical study of the Scriptures is in our age a duty, then we may safely say that history, having lost the power to speak and teach, is dumb upon all the questions that touch us to the quick. Criticism is a necessity imposed upon the mind of the Church — upon the Christian conscious-ness, if we prefer the phrase — by the very constitu-tion of the Church coöperating with the methods and apparatus of our time. Dogmatic speculation was the prime duty of the Church in the Nicene age. In no other way could the Christian reason have real con-versation and commerce with the organised know-ledge of the Mediterranean world; for that was philosophical and speculative.[1] But the organised knowledge of our age is scientific; its method is criti-cal; its objects, the original facts of Nature and His-tory; the consequence, an unsparing examination of all hypotheses, whether they date from day before yesterday or the most venerable antiquity. The Church, then, if she would have commerce with our time, even as the ancient Church had commerce with the ancient time, must take criticism with profound seriousness. Coquetry will not do. Even a left-handed marriage between authority and interpretation will not serve. Criticism is her prime duty. Through the duty lies the road to peace and power.

The sins of critics no more impair the authority of criticism than the sins of Churchmen impair the right of the Church to exist. It were easy, if it were worth our while, to draw up a catalogue of sins. Critics have set up cliques for purposes of mutual admiration.

[1] Make all allowance for the splendid scientific work of Alex-andria, yet this remains true. The mood of the great body of earnest men was not scientific but philosophical. Windelband, *Hist. of Philosophy*, pt. 2, ch. 2.

They have known too much. They have gone a-whoring after new things. They have invented a modern heresy — the heresy of contemporaneity. But enough of that, and more than enough. To what purpose is it to dwell upon the sins of individual critics, when it has been proved that criticism is a saving necessity laid upon us by the Lord of the Church? With or without our will, we must follow him.

The honour of Christ is at stake.[1] The act whereby the Reformation exalted the Bible above Tradition was one with the act whereby the Christian consciousness declared that there should be no vicar of Christ save Christ himself. The doctrine of justification through faith was proclaimed with one breath, and in the next the sovereignty and clearness of Holy Scripture.[2] That the soul should cast itself upon the Saviour's care, and that the Saviour's book should be brought close to the common life, and opened to the reading and the study of the laity, were things that went together. The direct knowledge of his person could not be separated from the free and first-hand study of his book. His right to be his own vicar drew after it the right of the Bible to be its own interpreter.[3] He who is for us the embodied Word of God

Honour of Christ.

Evangelical religion and criticism.

[1] As early as Wiclif the knowledge of Scripture was consecrated to the honour of Christ.

Lechler, *Wiclif*, I, pp. 469–473; II, pp. 265–267. Bengel repeatedly associated his Bible-work with the Saviour's honour. It is also to be observed that the eighteenth century, which laid the foundations of criticism, at the same time brought the humanity of our Lord into prominence. Dorner, *Person Christi*. (1853), II, pp. 907–915.

[2] Kaftan, *Truth of the Christian Religion*, Div. 1, ch. 3; Lipsius, *Dogmatik* (1893), pp. 139, 141–143, 149, 151, 155, 156.

[3] The Protestant doctrine regarding the " clearness " of Scripture did not mean that the Scripture could be mastered without study. What was really at stake was the right to study. Were

cannot be understood, according to his own mind, apart from a Bible-study that draws its inspiration and its strength from devotion to him, while it takes its methods from the historical spirit of our age.

Our study of the New Testament, therefore, ceasing to be dogmatic, has become historical and critical. But it need not, for that reason, cease to be devotional. "Critical" and "devotional" are adjectives which may live together quite as happily as "dogmatic" and "devotional." [1] The Word of God need not be less helpful, less rich in spiritual suggestion, because we know it in its history. We may gain a critical knowledge of nature without losing our sense of nature's beauty. The knowledge that the ground lines of the landscape are the result of a certain order of rock formation need not permanently impair the landscape's power to set us free from the cares that harass the unity of life. For a while that may be the case. But in the end the beauty will be more pervading and compelling because through it the earth tells the story of her struggles. Even so, the beauty of God's Word may be impaired for a time by our analytical study of the sources. But in the end its power to cheer our hearts and strengthen our purpose shall be the greater, by reason of our deeper knowledge of the history through which the being and beauty of God have been revealed.

"Critical" and "devotional."

Devotional element in criticism.

The very word "criticism," objectionable as it sounds to many, contains, when rightly taken, a deeply devotional element. For, to the student, it is

the laity to have the right of free Bible-study and free speech? Or was the Bible to be kept within the Tradition of the Church, — Tradition being a clerical monopoly?

[1] Leonardo da Vinci was not the less an artist by reason of his knowledge of anatomy. The antithesis between the critical and the devotional moods is not inherent.

a steady reminder that he must be on guard against reading his own thoughts into God's Word. The Bible-student of the old days, in good faith, carried into the Scriptures every conception that was dear to him, no matter where it came from. Thus Philo dressed Moses in the clothes of Plato and Aristotle. Thus the Popes transformed Peter the fisherman into the prince of the earth. In many ways the sacred text lay at the mercy of the devout interpreter. But the critical conception of the Scriptures makes the student reverent of the rights of the text. He is governed by the desire to know the original feeling and thought of the men of the Bible. He has a resolute purpose to permit no need of his own soul, no necessity of the Church, to force him one inch beyond the opinion which the text itself has given him. Surely, this is to give the highest possible honour to the Scriptures. Surely, if it can be said of any kind of consecrated work that to labour is to pray, then it may be said of patient, reverent, and fearless criticism.

Criticism has its inspiration. The credal period was inspired. Without it we should not have had our Bible. Without it we should not have had that common Christian consciousness which is the foundation of the idealising forces of our time. Our own critical age is no less inspired. For, without the historical interpretation, the Bible would cease to be our book of witness to the creative and saving unity of the divine life. We cannot go backward. The road into the Middle Ages is no thoroughfare of the Christian reason. At best, it is a by-path. In the stress and strain of the coming days, many, no doubt, will walk therein. None the less, it is a by-path. We know, unless History has wholly deceived us, we know that God's highway runs through a deeper, a more truly critical study of his Word.

The inspiration of criticism.

England and America.

It may be that England and America, now that Germany has marked out the road, have a work to do that Germany has not been able to do. The isolation of the academic life, necessary as it has been to the freedom of research, may have entailed a sort of blindness to some important aspects of the Scriptures. Possibly, the English and American scholars may see, through the grace of circumstance, what the German scholar has not seen.[1]

Criticism and the social movement.

It may be that the social movement of our age, while it brings in its train some grave dangers to sound thought,[2] shall bring a great blessing. The central idea of the Scriptures is the Kingdom of God. The dogmatic movement of the ancient and mediæval Church, going along with a deepening affection for the monastic ideal, sorely obscured that idea. But in our time it has shone forth afresh.[3] And it is pos-

---

[1] The Bible as a grand total may be waiting for a class of scholars who shall stand closer to the collective religious life both in its practical needs and in its social action. In England and America the pulpit and the chair are very close together, the result being that critical courage and thoroughness are harder to get. The scholar is apt to pay a heavy price for his freedom. Along with this goes the fact that the necessity of popularising the results of criticism is more pressing. At the same time, the situation is more nervous. The gain, however, is that the scholar has the chance to get an instinctive sense of the nature of religion on its collective and social side. This may fit him to appreciate certain undiscovered aspects of those Sacred Books, which are the products and records, not of a school, but of a religious community.

[2] Sociology is a great help to sound theology, but a poor, if not perilous, substitute for it. Did we not know that the present is the preparation for a better future, we should look upon the low ebb of speculative interest in the Churches as a bad sign. In many a case already the critical passion, lacking speculation, has slipped into naturalism.

[3] Lipsius, *Dogmatik*, pp. 822, 840; Nitzsch, *Dogmatik*, p. 26.

sible that the social movement may bring us into a common mood with the Bible, so that we shall be able to study it with instinctive sympathy.[1]

However that may be, we know our duty. The Word of God has been unbound, set free from the shackles that human opinion had put upon it. The scholar will strengthen himself with the prayer that, through his work, the Word of the Lord may have free course and be glorified (2 Thess. 3 : 1); so that the Bible may commend itself to reasoning and reverent men as God's book of final values for all who would live nobly.

[1] Cheyne, *Jeremiah, His Life and Times*, p. 12.

By special arrangement with a churchman interested in modern Bible study as laying the surest foundations for faith in Jesus Christ the Word of God, we have the pleasure of placing in your hands a complimentary copy of Dr. Nash's "Higher Criticism of the New Testament."

THE MACMILLAN COMPANY,
64-66 Fifth Avenue, New York.

INDEX

Allegory: opposed to historical nature of revelation, 30; universal tendency in ancient days, 31; overcome, 177, 178.

"Apostolic Age": significance of the title, 179.

Augustine: opinions concerning relation of the Church to the Bible, 33, n. 1.

Authority: an authoritative interpretation necessary in antiquity, 32; its quality not in keeping with Scripture, 45–49; involves the Church in self-contradiction, 50–52.

Bauer, B., 170, n. 1.

Baur, F. C., 127; ushers in the new principle in criticism, 128; idea of conflict in primitive Christianity, 129–130.

Bede, 43, n. 2.

Bengel, 91–92.

Bible: not passive in the critical process, 17–19; its own character a main cause, 20–26; the Church's standard, 27; not a sacerdotal book, 28–29; isolated, 38–41; first-hand knowledge of Scriptures not possible in Middle Ages, 44; growing reverence for Scripture, 50, 53; conflict with Tradition, 51, 54; its own interpreter, 75–76; thrown open to observation, 89; isolation overcome, 103; supremacy of Scriptures de-

mands historical interpretation, 105.

Bible-study: since second century, 9; part of higher culture, 3–4.

Bleek, 166–167.

Boniface VIII states the claims of the Papacy, 55.

Bradford, 75.

Bretschneider, 105, n. 2, 114.

Canon: relation to Bible-study, 10, n. 1; above investigation, 42; becomes the subject of historical study, 103–104.

Cassiodorus, 41, n. 1.

Change, idea of: had no place in ancient view of Scriptures, 42, 100.

Chillingworth, 63.

Christ, person of: the Saviour and his book, 25; historical study of our time contrasted with speculation of Nicene Age, 144–145; honour of Christ and criticism, 150–151, 179, 183.

Church, relation to Scripture, 17–19, 27, 32–34, 53.

Colet defends literal interpretation, 63.

Comte, 146.

Conservatism: that of Germany contrasted with conservatism in England and America, 159–161.

Credner, 114.

Criticism: waste attending it, 8;

189

New Testament Handbooks

EDITED BY

SHAILER MATHEWS

PROFESSOR OF NEW TESTAMENT HISTORY AND INTERPRETATION
IN THE UNIVERSITY OF CHICAGO

Cloth   16mo   75 cents net each

THE MACMILLAN COMPANY

64-66 Fifth Avenue, New York

The Work of Preaching

A BOOK FOR THE CLASSROOM AND STUDY

By ARTHUR L. HOYT, D.D.

PROFESSOR OF HOMILETICS AND SOCIOLOGY IN THE AUBURN THEOLOGICAL SEMINARY

Cloth   12mo $1.50 net

"It furnishes hints, counsels, helps, directions, and conclusions based on the questions of students, the experience of the author, on the sage advice of other teachers, and on independent study, . . . applicable to the needs of the hour." — *Western Christian Advocate.*

Representative Modern Preachers

By LEWIS O. BRASTOW, D.D.

PROFESSOR OF PRACTICAL THEOLOGY, YALE UNIVERSITY

Cloth   12mo $1.50 net

Careful critical estimates of preachers who have prominently represented different schools of preaching during the last century; whose skill and force in presenting the truth have won the right to a special hearing.

THE MACMILLAN COMPANY

64–66 Fifth Avenue, New York